How to Use This Book

Look for these special features in this book:

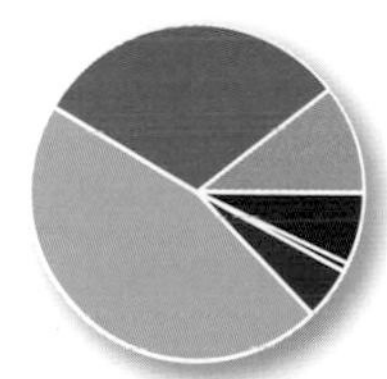

SIDEBARS, **CHARTS**, **GRAPHS**, and original **MAPS** expand your understanding of what's being discussed—and also make useful sources for classroom reports.

FAQs answer common **F**requently **A**sked **Q**uestions about people, places, and things.

WOW FACTORS offer "Who knew?" facts to keep you thinking.

TRAVEL GUIDE gives you tips on exploring the state—either in person or right from your chair!

PROJECT ROOM provides fun ideas for school assignments and incredible research projects. Plus, there's a guide to primary sources—what they are and how to cite them.

Please note: All statistics are as up-to-date as possible at the time of publication.

Consultants: Lynn Fichter, Department of Geology and Environmental Science, James Madison University; George H. Gilliam, Chair of the Miller Center Forum and Assistant Director of Public Affairs, University of Virginia Miller Center of Public Affairs; William Loren Katz

Book production by The Design Lab

Library of Congress Cataloging-in-Publication Data
Kent, Deborah.
Virginia / by Deborah Kent.
p. cm.—(America the beautiful. Third series)
Includes bibliographical references and index.
ISBN-13: 978-0-531-18581-0
ISBN-10: 0-531-18581-8
1. Virginia—Juvenile literature. I. Title. II. Series.
F226.3.K46 2008
975.5—dc22 2007028463

1 2 3 4 5 6 7 8 9 10 R 18 17 16 15 14 13 12 11 10 09

Virginia

BY DEBORAH KENT

Third Series

Children's Press®
An Imprint of Scholastic Inc.
New York ★ Toronto ★ London ★ Auckland ★ Sydney
Mexico City ★ New Delhi ★ Hong Kong
Danbury, Connecticut

CONTENTS

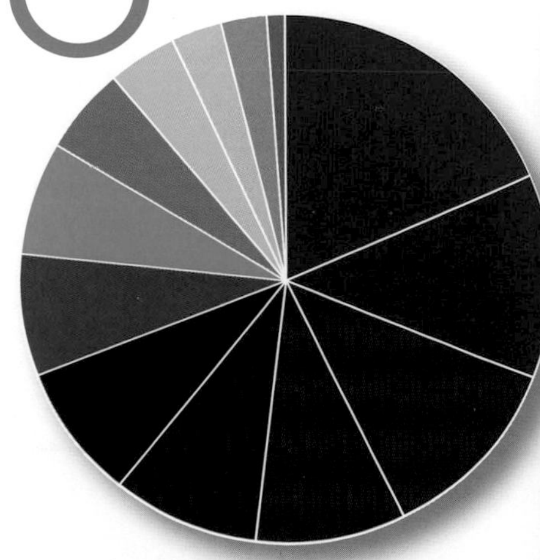

OHIO

PENNSYLVANIA

0 50
Miles

Arlington National Cemetery

Assateague Island National Seashore

N.J.

MARYLAND

DELAWARE

Mount Vernon Estate and Gardens

Shenandoah Valley Caverns

Washington, D.C.

ARLINGTON

WEST VIRGINIA

Mountains

Shenandoah

Potomac

Monticello

CHARLOTTESVILLE

Edgar Allan Poe Museum

Pamunkey Indian Museum

Chesapeake Bay

Black History Museum and Cultural Center

KENTUCKY

VIRGINIA

RICHMOND

Appalachian

ROANOKE

Virginia State Capitol

James

PJ's Carousel Collection

Booker T. Washington National Monument

Roanoke

Historical Appomattox Court House National Historic Park

NEWPORT NEWS

NORFOLK

Yorktown Victory Center

VIRGINIA BEACH

TENNESSEE

Jamestown Settlement

NORTH CAROLINA

Great Dismal Swamp National Wildlife Refuge

ATLANTIC OCEAN

SOUTH CAROLINA

QUICK FACTS

State capital: Richmond
Largest city: Virginia Beach
Total area: 42,774 square miles (110,784 sq km); 35th
Highest point: Mount Rogers at 5,722 feet (1,744 m)
Lowest point: Sea level along the Atlantic Ocean

CONNECTICUT

NEW YORK

Welcome to Virginia!

HOW DID VIRGINIA GET ITS NAME?

VIRGINIA

In 1584, European nations were busily carving out territories in North America. Queen Elizabeth I of England asked an adventurer named Sir Walter Raleigh (sometimes spelled Ralegh, his preferred spelling) to start colonies on the continent's southeastern coast. Looking at a map, Raleigh gave the name Virginia to the vast new land across the Atlantic. This territory sprawled from New England to Florida, and reached westward all the way to the Mississippi River. He chose the name Virginia in honor of Queen Elizabeth. Because she never married, Elizabeth was sometimes called the "Virgin Queen." Eventually, Virginia was divided into several states. One of them is the state we know today as Virginia.

READ ABOUT

Lace Falls near the Natural Bridge rock formation

CHAPTER ONE

LAND

★

IF YOU COME FROM VIRGINIA, YOU MIGHT LIVE NEAR A COALFIELD IN THE MOUNTAINS. You might live next to a horse farm on a rolling plain. Your house might even be on an island in Chesapeake Bay. Virginia is a medium-sized state, but it has a dazzling variety of landscapes. Much of Virginia's 42,774 square miles (110,784 square kilometers) lies at sea level, with the lowest point along the Atlantic Ocean. Yet Virginia's highest point, Mount Rogers, soars to 5,722 feet (1,744 meters).

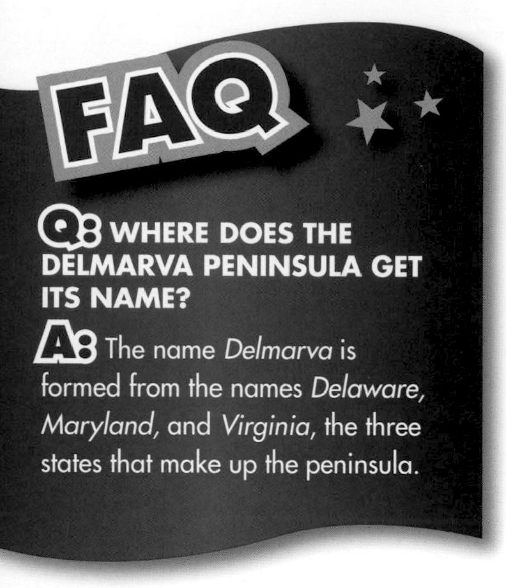

Q8 WHERE DOES THE DELMARVA PENINSULA GET ITS NAME?

A8 The name *Delmarva* is formed from the names *Delaware, Maryland,* and *Virginia,* the three states that make up the peninsula.

BORDERS

On a map of the United States, Virginia lies in the middle of the Atlantic Coast. It is perched about midway between Maine to the north and Florida to the south. Virginia shares boundaries with five other states. At its western tip it borders Kentucky. Virginia's northwestern border forms a gentle curve around the edge of West Virginia. Due north, across the Potomac River, is Maryland. Virginia's southern border is almost ruler straight. This border divides Virginia from North Carolina, and from Tennessee in the far west.

Along the east coast of Virginia lies Chesapeake Bay, a long arm of the Atlantic Ocean. On the east side of the bay is the Delmarva Peninsula, sometimes called the Eastern Shore. Delaware and part of Maryland occupy most of the peninsula, but the southern tip of the peninsula is part of Virginia. The waters of Chesapeake Bay completely separate this sliver of Virginia from the rest of the state.

Virginia Geo-Facts

Along with the state's geographical highlights, this chart ranks Virginia's land, water, and total area compared to all other states.

Total area; rank	42,774 square miles (110,784 sq km); 35th
Land; rank	39,594 square miles (102,548 sq km); 37th
Water; rank	3,180 square miles (8,236 sq km); 15th
Inland water; rank	1,006 square miles (2,606 sq km); 22nd
Coastal water; rank	1,728 square miles (4,475 sq km); 5th
Territorial water; rank	446 square miles (1,155 sq km); 16th
Geographic center	5 miles (8 km) southwest of Buckingham
Longitude	75° 13′ W to 83° 37′ W
Latitude	36° 31′ N to 39° 37′ N
Highest point	Mount Rogers at 5,722 feet (1,744 m)
Lowest point	Sea level along the Atlantic Ocean
Largest city	Virginia Beach
Longest river	James River, 340 miles (547 km)

Source: U.S. Census Bureau

Virginia may be a medium-sized state, but it has more coastline than 45 other states.

LAND REGIONS

On a map, the state of Virginia is shaped roughly like a squashed triangle. The land itself slopes downward from west to east. The westernmost part of the state has mountains and deep valleys. The eastern side of the triangle lies along the Atlantic Ocean. From west to east, Virginia's five major

Virginia Topography

Use the color-coded elevation chart to see on the map Virginia's high points (dark red to orange) and low points (green to dark green). Elevation is measured as the distance above or below sea level.

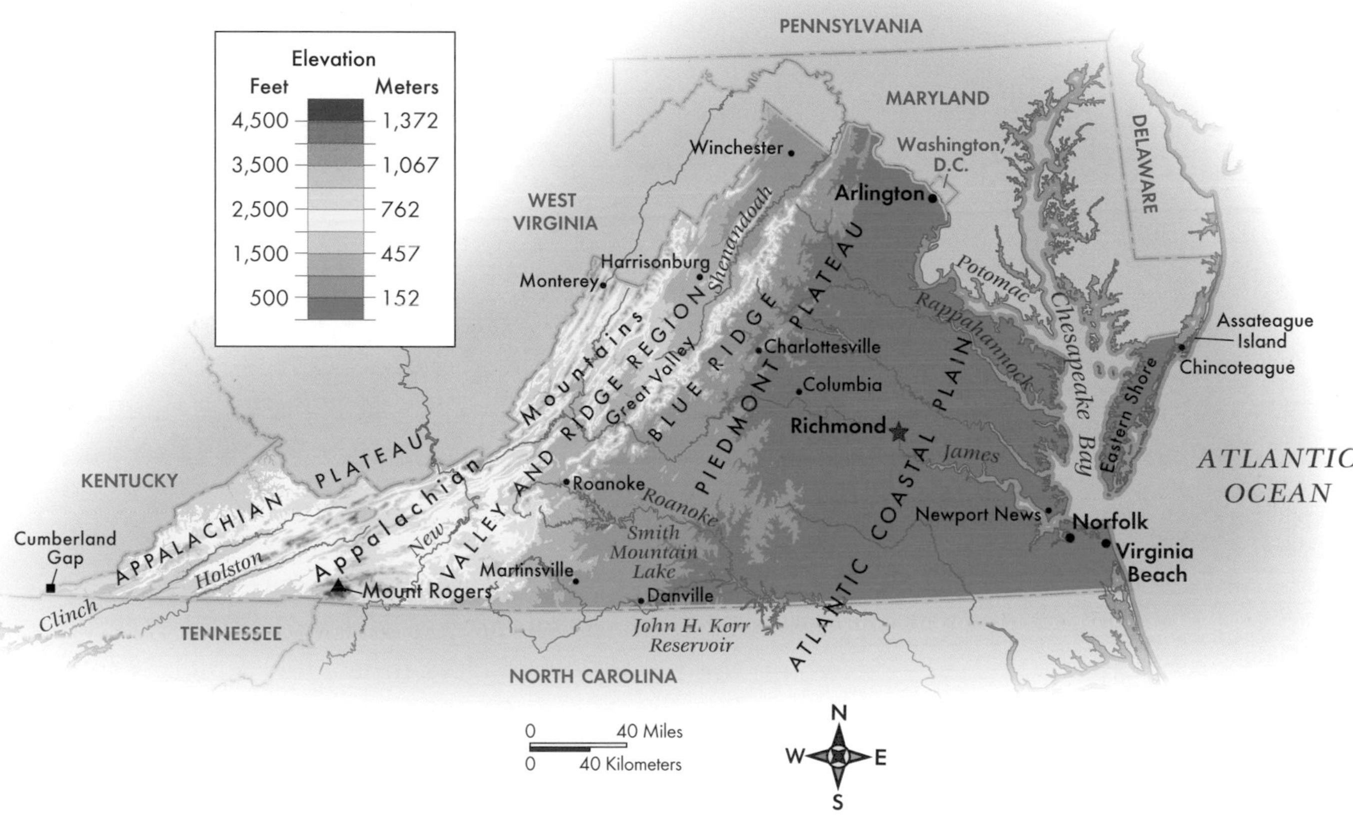

land regions are the Appalachian Plateau, Valley and Ridge, Blue Ridge, Piedmont, and Coastal Plain.

Appalachian Plateau

Virginia's far western tip is part of the rugged Appalachian Plateau. Deep valleys, so bent that roads are full of twists and turns, surround round-topped hills. Some mountains in this area are 3,000 feet (900 m) high. Beneath the Appalachian Plateau stretch fields of coal.

A hiker in Shenandoah Valley National Park

Valley and Ridge

The Valley and Ridge is a series of mountain ridges separated by parallel valleys. The valleys are carved where the underlying rock is limestone, which is soft. The ridges are made of hard rock that does not erode as easily. The largest valley is the Shenandoah, made famous by the 19th-century folk song "Oh Shenandoah." The tumbling Shenandoah River drains through the beautiful valley. The Shenandoah Valley is filled with rich farmland because limestone is good for soil.

The Valley and Ridge is known for its spectacular rock formations. The limestone is sculpted into towering columns and great, arching bridges. Here and there, waterfalls plunge over steep cliffs. The mountains are honeycombed with caves, created by the action of underground streams. In some places, hot springs bubble to the surface.

FOSSIL FUEL

Coal is known as a fossil fuel because it is formed from the fossilized remains of ancient plants and animals. Over millions of years, layers of earth and rock piled up on these remains. The heat and pressure turned them into coal.

Blue Ridge

The Blue Ridge mountain range is much older and more rugged looking than its neighbor, the Valley and Ridge. The rocks in the Blue Ridge are between 700 million and 1 billion years old. These include some of the oldest rocks in eastern North America. These rocks generally make poor soil, and farming never got a foothold in this region.

The Blue Ridge Mountains are named for the bluish mist that sometimes hangs above them. The Blue Ridge region contains not only these mountains but also some generally flat land to the east, including the cities of Charlottesville, Orange, Culpeper, and Warrenton.

Piedmont Plateau

East of the Blue Ridge, the land descends to a rolling plateau called the Piedmont. At the northern edge of the state, the Piedmont is about 40 miles (64 kilometers) wide. It broadens as it reaches southward, until it is some 185 miles (298 km) wide when it enters North Carolina. The Piedmont has many scenic lakes and wooded areas.

Along the eastern rim of the Piedmont, rivers tumble over rocky shelves to a level plain below. The line where the land makes this sharp descent is called the Fall Line. It marks the division between the Piedmont and the Coastal Plain.

A kayaker gets ready for the Potomac.

Coastal Plain

The Coastal Plain, also known as the Tidewater, is part of a long strip of land that runs from New Jersey to Florida. In Virginia, four rivers roll across the Coastal Plain to Chesapeake Bay. From north to south, these rivers are the Potomac, the Rappahannock,

SEE IT HERE!

THE GREAT DISMAL SWAMP

To nature lovers, there is nothing dismal about the vast wetland known as the Great Dismal Swamp. It is a splendid place to see birds and animals in their natural surroundings. The Great Dismal Swamp sprawls over 111,000 acres (45,000 hectares) in Virginia and North Carolina. Ninety-six species of birds nest there, and many others pass through during spring and fall migrations.

the York, and the James. As the tide rises in the bay, salt water flows into the river mouths. These rivers rise with the tides as far west as the Fall Line.

The four rivers break Virginia's Tidewater into three long peninsulas that stretch toward the bay like the tines of a fork. A sprawling wetland called the Great Dismal Swamp covers Virginia's southeastern corner and spreads into North Carolina.

The Eastern Shore is also part of the Coastal Plain. For millions of years, coastal currents have picked up sand and moved it around. It collected in long sandbars. Over time, these sandbars grew into a chain of islands extending along the Eastern Shore peninsula to the mouth of Chesapeake Bay. Virginia shares Assateague Island with Maryland. Islands belonging entirely to Virginia include Chincoteague, Tangier, and Fisherman.

CLIMATE

Virginia's climate varies widely from one part of the state to another. Summers in the Tidewater are warm and humid. In the mountains, summer temperatures are cool and pleasant. The Tidewater enjoys mild winters, with an average of 10 inches (25 centimeters) of snowfall. Snowfall in the mountains averages about 25 inches (64 cm) per year, and winters can be long and harsh.

Virginia's climate variations greatly affect farmers. The growing season in the mountains is about 150 days

Weather Report

TEMPERATURE 110°F

TEMPERATURE -30°F

This chart shows record temperatures (high and low) for the state, as well as average temperatures (July and January) and average annual precipitation.

Record high temperature . . . . 110°F (43°C) at Columbia on July 5, 1900, and Balcony Falls on July 15, 1954

Record low temperature . . . .–30°F (–34°C) at Monterey on February 10, 1899, and Mountain Lake Biological Station on January 22, 1985

Average July temperature . . . . 78°F (26°C)

Average January temperature . . . . 36°F (2°C)

Average yearly precipitation . . . . 43 inches (109 cm)

Source: National Climatic Data Center, NESDIS, NOAA, U.S. Dept. of Commerce

long. This means that farmers in the Appalachian Plateau and the Blue Ridge areas can expect about 150 frost-free days per year. The Tidewater, on the other hand, has a growing season of about 240 days annually.

Full-scale hurricanes seldom strike Virginia, although major tropical storms hit about every five years. Tornadoes occur an average of seven times a year in Virginia. In 1993, a record 28 tornadoes whipped across the state!

THE ASSAULT OF FLOYD

In September 1999, tropical storm Floyd lashed Virginia's Tidewater region. Some 300,000 people lost electricity, many for up to six days. High winds uprooted trees. Heavy rains caused flooding that closed highways. Flash floods burst two dams on the Rappahannock River. Damage in Virginia was estimated at $101 million.

PLANT LIFE

Each of Virginia's regions presents a unique environment, each with its own assortment of plant species. Sixteen kinds of sea grass grow in the shallow waters along Chesapeake Bay and its islands. The Piedmont's wooded areas are thick with hardwood trees such as white oak, red oak, yellow poplar, and beech.

Red spruce grows on the highest mountains in western Virginia. Lower down grow beech, yellow birch, and sugar maples. Many plants grow on the forest floor, including medicinal plants such as ginseng and goldenseal.

Loblolly pine trees in a salt marsh on Assateague Island

Virginia National Park Areas

This map shows some of Virginia's national parks, monuments, preserves, and other areas protected by the National Park Service.

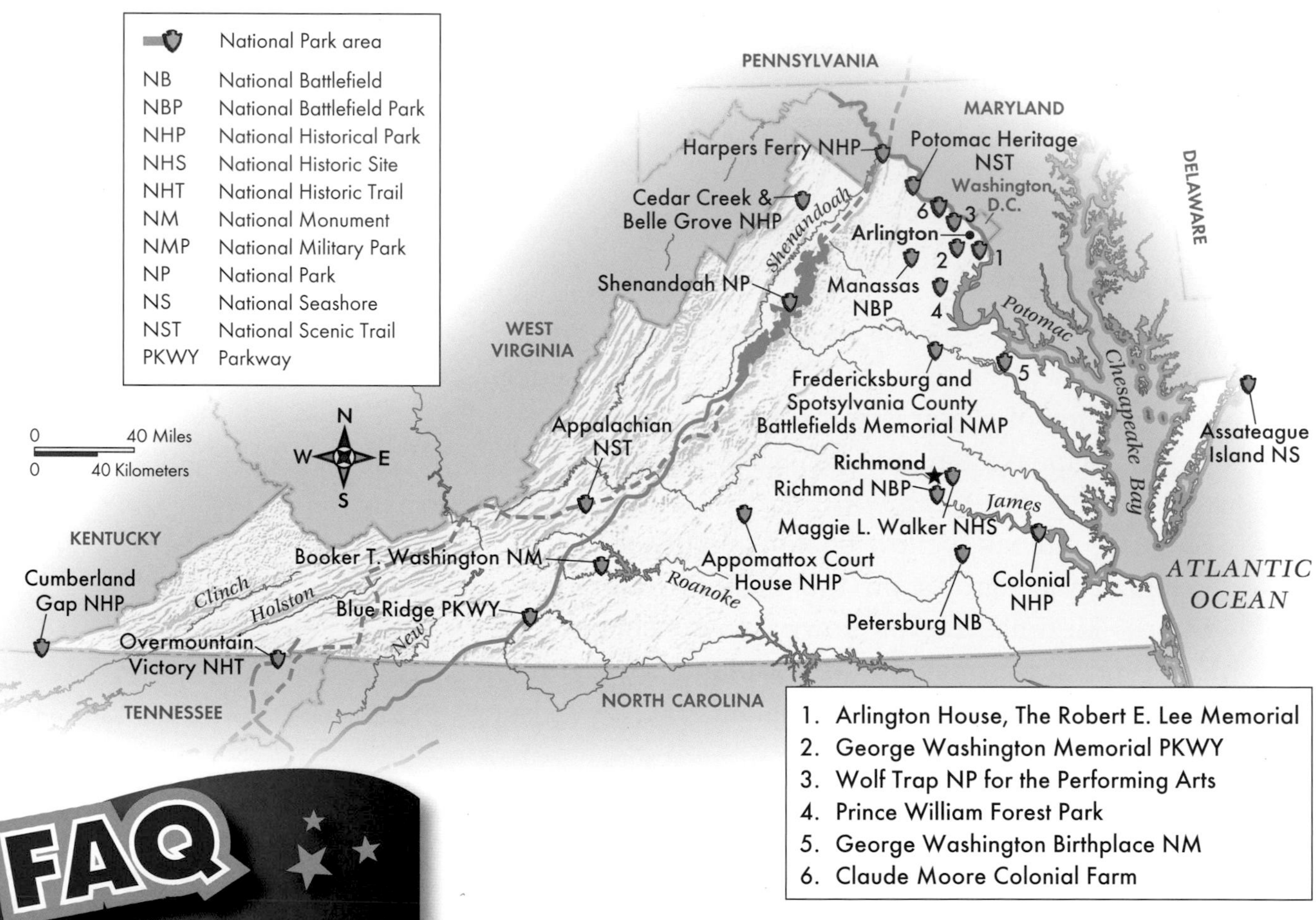

FAQ

Q8 ARE THERE ANY POISONOUS SNAKES IN VIRGINIA?

A8 Virginia has four species of poisonous snakes. They are the copperhead, the cottonmouth or water moccasin, and two kinds of rattlesnakes—the timber rattler and the canebrake rattler.

ANIMAL LIFE

The sea grasses along Virginia's shore provide a habitat for oysters, blue crabs, squid, and many kinds of fish. Striped bass, summer flounder, weakfish, bluefish, and menhaden swim in the bay and enter Virginia's rivers when the tide rises. Sandpipers, plovers, gulls, and ospreys nest along the shores. Porpoises and sea turtles often swim at the southern end of Chesapeake Bay.

A wildlife researcher walks among the laughing gulls on Wreck Island.

The woodlands of the Piedmont and western Virginia are home to many mammals and birds. Beavers dam streams, and white-tailed deer browse on the underbrush. In the spring, the woods are loud with the voices of songbirds.

WORDS TO KNOW

endangered *in danger of becoming extinct*

threatened *likely to become endangered in the foreseeable future*

VIRGINIA'S ENDANGERED SPECIES

Sixty-three **endangered** and **threatened** species of plants and animals survive in Virginia. Endangered animals include the Virginia big-eared bat, the Shenandoah salamander, and the Delmarva Peninsula fox squirrel. Among Virginia's endangered plants are the sensitive joint-vetch, the shale barren rockcress, the Virginia round-leaf birch, and the smooth coneflower.

Delmarva Peninsula fox squirrel

CARING FOR THE LAND

"To everyone, especially to those who live in narrow streets where automobiles are thicker than ants in an ant-hill . . . we say 'Come to this beautiful Blue Ridge area for recreation and interesting knowledge,'" said park engineer James R. Lassiter at the dedication of Shenandoah National Park in 1936. "You will carry away . . . a little more strength, a little more wisdom, a little more happiness than you brought with you." Some 24,000 Virginians raised money to purchase 300 square miles (855 sq km) of land in the Blue Ridge Mountains for the creation of the park. The park was not established in a wilderness area. Much of the land had been used for farms and homes for many years. Signs of human activity were cleared away. Little by little, wilderness reclaimed the land.

WORD TO KNOW

pesticides *any chemicals or biological agents used to kill plant or animal pests*

Today, Virginia faces many pressures from a rapidly growing population. Woodlands are cleared for housing developments. Exhaust fumes from millions of automobiles pollute the air. Pollution from factories and farm **pesticides** has seeped into Virginia's rivers and streams. Fish and shellfish populations in Chesapeake Bay have dwindled.

Housing developments like this one near Manassas have been built in areas that used to be forests.

Many Virginians are working to reverse the damage. As they did in the 1930s, they are trying to reclaim land and water resources.

In many places, oil-tainted rainwater runs off asphalt parking lots and finds its way into streams and rivers. Virginia's Stafford and Fairfax counties have found a way to reduce this pollution. The counties created green areas of earth and gravel around many large parking lots. The earth and gravel filter about 95 percent of the oil and other harmful substances out of the rainwater. Eventually, clean water reaches the Potomac and Rappahannock rivers and flows from there to Chesapeake Bay.

THE EAGLE LADY

In 1965, Elizabeth Speer Hartwell (1924–2000) led a successful campaign to block development on Mason Neck in Fairfax County. The area provided nesting grounds for the last bald eagles in northern Virginia. Angry developers nicknamed her "the Eagle Lady," but she carried the nickname proudly. Hartwell helped preserve about 5,000 acres (2,023 ha) of woods and wetlands on the Mason Neck Peninsula. Want to know more? See www.hartwellfund.com

THINK ABOUT IT!

Logging in National Forests

Virginia's George Washington and Jefferson national forests comprise 1.7 million acres (688,000 ha) of timber. In 2005, new federal laws made it easier for timber companies to log in national forests without regard for the impact on the environment. In Virginia, concerned groups and individuals went into action. They contacted representatives in Congress and worked to educate the public about the value of the forests and the new threat to their well-being. In a brochure titled *Forests for the Future*, they explained that the George Washington National Forest "harbors many natural and cultural resources often not available or protected on private lands, including clean water for fishing and drinking, wildlife habitat for game and non-game species, maturing native forests, backcountry recreation, scenic views, and much more. . . . Unfortunately, in the past the Forest Service has too often focused on logging and road-building over these other values. . . . The time has come to restore balance."

READ ABOUT

Archaeologists Lynn and Joseph McAvoy working at Cactus Hill

c. 15,000 BCE ▲
The first people enter Virginia

c. 12,000 BCE
The Archaic culture develops

c. 9800 BCE
People begin living in Daugherty's Cave in today's western Virginia

CHAPTER TWO

FIRST PEOPLE

★

SOME OF THE OLDEST HUMAN BONES IN EASTERN NORTH AMERICA WERE FOUND IN SOUTHERN VIRGINIA. Scientists say the bones' age proves that peoplc lived in Virginia about 15,000 BCE. These first Virginians probably descended from people who crossed into North America from Asia over a land bridge that once connected the two continents.

c. 1200 BCE
People begin settling in villages

c. 1600s
About 50,000 people live in what is now Virginia

◂ early 1600s
Wahunsunacock unites 32 Powhatan groups

An early hunter returns to a campsite with food for his group.

PALEO-INDIANS

When the first humans reached Virginia, vast sheets of ice called glaciers covered parts of today's United States. The ice did not reach Virginia, but it made the climate much colder than it is today. Caribou, moose, and elk roamed over open grasslands. There were also bison and huge elephant-like creatures called mastodons.

Archaeologists call the earliest Virginians Paleo-Indians. The Paleo-Indians were always on the move, following herds of game animals. Archaeologists have found spear points, scrapers, drills, and many other stone tools that the Paleo-Indians left behind. By studying these tools and other ancient clues, such as mastodon bones, archaeologists know that the earliest Virginians hunted using stone-headed spears. They often made spear points from a yellow stone called jasper. Jasper chips easily when it is struck with another stone. These ancient people also gathered wild roots, berries, and nuts to eat.

WORD TO KNOW

archaeologists *people who study the remains of past human societies*

Stone spear points

Native American Peoples

(Before European Contact)

This map shows the general area of Native American peoples before European settlers arrived.

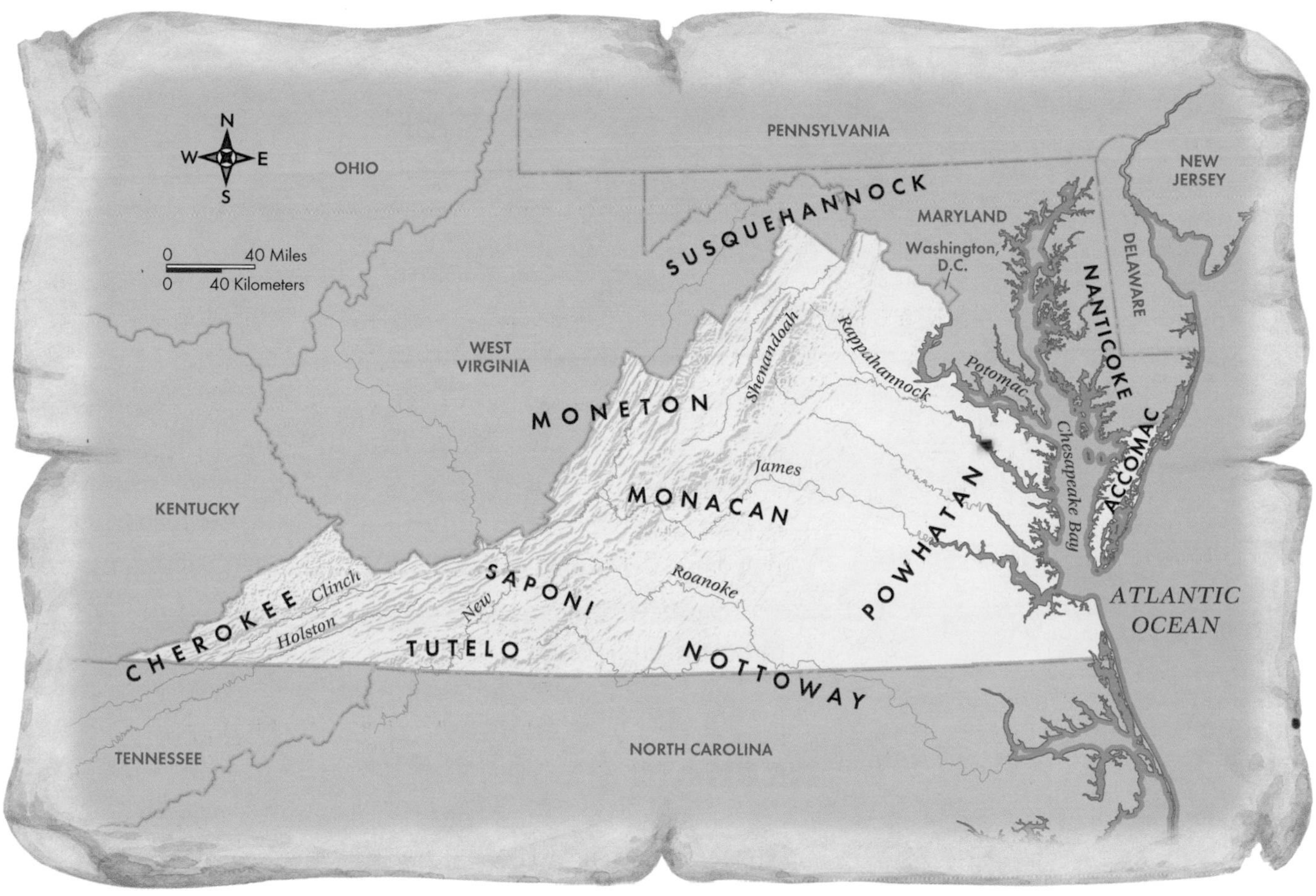

By about 12,000 BCE, the climate in North America began to grow warmer. The glaciers slowly melted away. Water from the melting ice caused the sea level to rise. The rising sea covered a wide shelf of coastal land.

Scientists are not entirely sure why the mastodon died out.

Daugherty's Cave in western Virginia was inhabited for more than 10,000 years! People lived there from about 9800 BCE until around 1600 CE.

The warming climate and melting ice led to other changes. In the land that is now Virginia, grasslands gave way to forests of evergreen and hardwood trees. The human population grew. Increased hunting may have reduced the herds of mastodons and other large game animals. For reasons scientists do not clearly understand, these animals soon became extinct.

ARCHAIC PEOPLE

As the climate warmed, deer and small game became plentiful. People lived in caves during the winter and followed game during the summer. Archaeologists refer to the people of this period as the Archaic People.

During the Archaic period, life in Virginia underwent many changes. People began to plant squash, sunflowers, and other food crops. They also discovered how to carve cooking pots and storage vessels from a soft stone called soapstone.

Because they were now raising some of their food, people lived in one place for months at a time. Groups of about 50 people formed small settlements. They developed elaborate beliefs about an unseen world of spirits. They believed that spirits lived in every natural object—in the rocks, streams, clouds, and mountains. The sun spirit provided light and warmth. The cloud spirit brought life-giving rain. Hunters tried to please the spirits of the deer, turkey, and other game animals. If the spirits were happy, the animals would come back.

WOODLAND PEOPLE

By about 1200 BCE, the Woodland culture had developed. A chief or head man now led each village. Around this time, people also learned to dig clay from riverbanks and shape it into pots, bowls, and other containers. After they dried in the sun, the vessels were heated in a fire pit. The intense heat strengthened the dried clay. These pottery vessels were much more practical than the earlier ones made of soapstone.

Woodland pottery

Some groups in western and central Virginia built burial mounds of earth and clay for important people such as chiefs and great warriors. Often they were laid to rest with spear points, axes, jewelry, and other valuable objects. The villagers believed that these objects would help the dead person on his or her journey in the spirit world.

During this period, which lasted until about 1600 CE, people became highly skilled at making canoes. They hollowed out a log by burning and carving it. They traveled by canoe through Virginia's network of rivers and streams. With canoes, they could trade with people outside their own neighborhoods. Traders from the south

SEE IT HERE!

WOLF CREEK INDIAN VILLAGE

Would you like to watch an arrowhead being made? Would you like to try your hand at molding a pottery bowl or weaving a straw mat? A community from about the year 1250 has been reconstructed at Wolf Creek Indian Village near Bastian in southwestern Virginia. The staff demonstrates many early Native crafts and offers visitors the chance to get some hands-on experience. A museum on the grounds displays tools, weapons, and other objects found nearby.

sometimes visited Virginia, and people from Virginia probably traveled south. Beaded necklaces, copper bracelets, and beautifully woven blankets from as far away as Mexico have been found at sites in Virginia. The Woodland people also began to plant new crops that came from Mexico, including tobacco and gourds.

By the year 1600, about 50,000 people lived in what is now Virginia. These people belonged to several different groups. Although many of the groups still moved from place to place, each had its own territory.

CHEROKEES

In 1600, Cherokee villages were scattered throughout western North Carolina, eastern Tennessee, northern Georgia, and the western tip of Virginia. Cherokees built their houses by weaving slender branches between poles set into the ground. They plastered the outside walls with clay, which helped to keep out the rain. In the center of the house was a hearth. Smoke escaped through a hole in the roof.

Cherokee basket

Cherokees traced their families through their mothers. When a man married a Cherokee woman, he moved into her mother's house. Children were members of their mother's families. Their mother's belongings eventually passed to them.

A Cherokee man proved his worth by courage on the battlefield or in competitive games. Cherokees played a ball game similar to today's lacrosse. The game was so rough that it was thought of as a kind of warfare.

PEOPLE OF THE PIEDMONT

Several groups lived in Virginia's Piedmont region. Manahoacs lived along the Rappahannock River. Monacans lived above the Fall Line on the James River. Villages of Occaneechis and Saponis were scattered along the Roanoke River.

Archaeologists don't know much about the Piedmont peoples. Manahoacs and Monacans were friendly toward one another. Eventually, these two groups combined.

In the 1670s, a German traveler visited the Saponi people. He was one of the first Europeans to meet them. "This nation is governed by an absolute monarch," he wrote. "The people [are] of a high stature, warlike and rich. I saw great stores of pearls in their little temples, which they . . . hold in as great esteem as we do." The same traveler described an unusual Saponi custom. When a visitor arrived, his host bound him with rope as if he were a prisoner. After a few minutes, the guest was untied and all was well. This custom seemed to be a way Saponis showed their power to friends as well as enemies.

Jewelry made of shells

Occaneechis were great traders. People traveled hundreds of miles to trade jewelry, pottery, weapons, and other goods at an Occaneechi market center. To keep track of accounts, Occaneechis used a complicated system of knots on lengths of string. Occaneechi served as a common language for the peoples of the region.

THE RISE OF POWHATANS

In 1600, about 14,000 to 21,000 Native Americans lived on the Coastal Plain of today's Virginia. Most belonged to a group of peoples called Algonquians. The Algonquian groups had similar customs and beliefs. Although their

MINI-BIO

WAHUNSUNACOCK: VIRGINIA'S EMPEROR

Through warfare and persuasion, Chief Wahunsunacock (1547?–1618?) created an empire in eastern Virginia. Thirty-two groups, with about 150 villages, were under his control. Wahunsunacock (sometimes called Chief Powhatan) lived at the town of Tenakomakah (the present-day Tidewater area). The English explorer John Smith described him as "a tall well-proportioned man, with a sour look, his head somewhat gray, . . . his age near 60; of a very able and hard body to endure any labor."

Want to know more? See http://virginiaindians.pwnet.org/history/1600s.php

languages were quite different, some words shared a common root.

In the early 1600s, about 32 Algonquian tribes were united under a single chief named Wahunsunacock. His people referred to him as the *powhatan*, or "leader." The people of his chiefdom are often called Powhatans.

Wahunsunacock protected the villages of his chiefdom from attack by other groups. In return for this protection, he demanded tribute. He required his subjects to bring him as much as 80 percent of the game they killed and the fish they caught.

Most Powhatan towns were built near rivers and had about 30 houses. Houses were oval in shape, with a low, narrow doorway. The frame was made from bent saplings and covered with straw mats.

Powhatan women wore long deerskin skirts, often covered in front with a fringed apron. Usually, they wore their hair in a single thick braid down their backs. For special occasions, they put on bracelets, necklaces, and earrings. In warm weather, men wore a simple **breechcloth** belted around the waist. They shaved the right side of their heads and let the hair on the left side grow long. During the winter, both men and women wore long fur cloaks. Girls dressed much like their mothers, and boys like their fathers.

WORD TO KNOW

breechcloth *a garment worn by a man over his lower body*

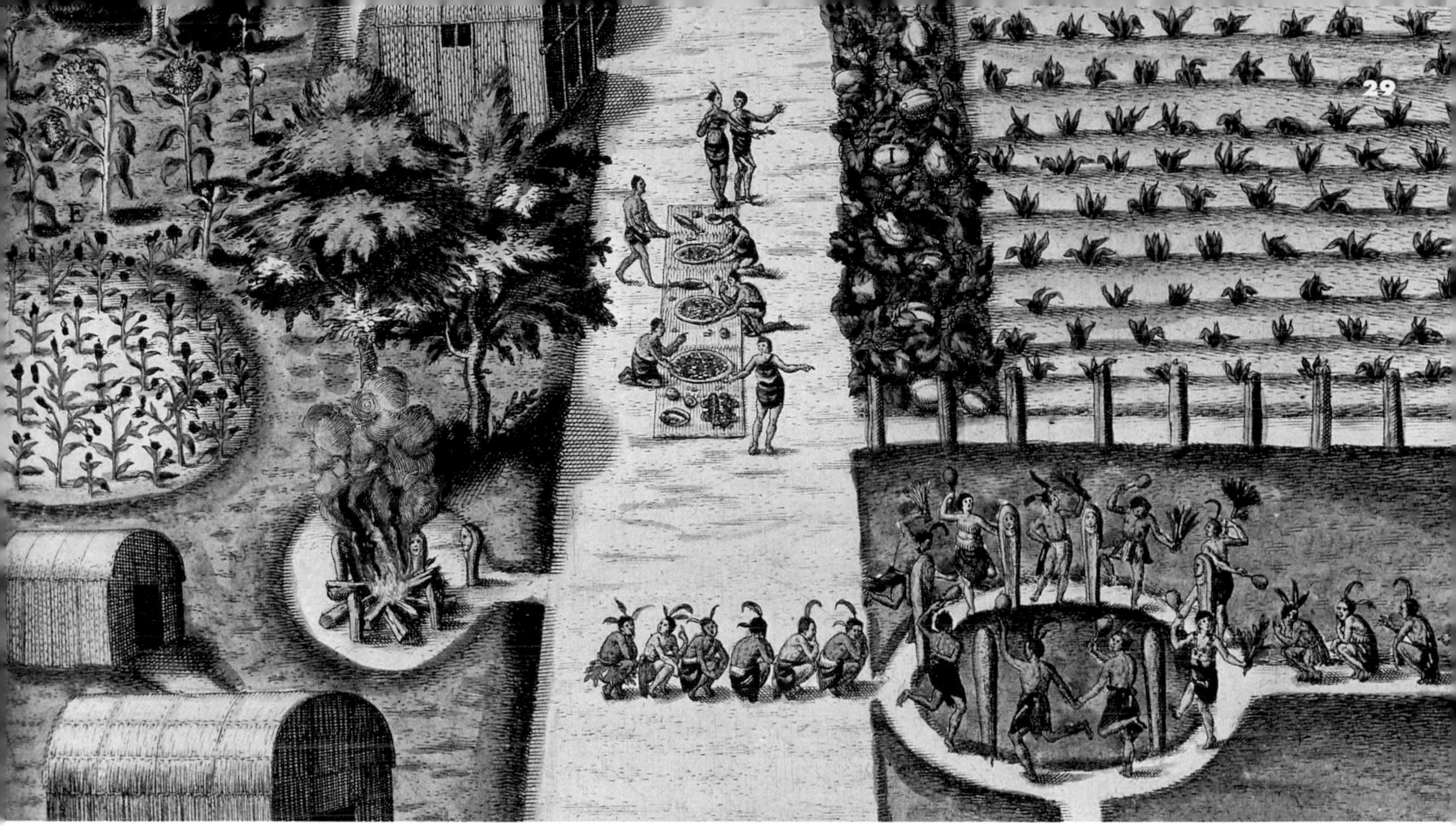

This painting, *The Towne of Secota*, shows people cooking and growing crops in an Algonquian village in Virginia.

MEN'S WORK AND WOMEN'S WORK

From early childhood, Powhatan boys learned to hunt. Their fathers and uncles taught them to stalk game and to shoot arrows from a bow. Boys were also expected to become brave warriors. At about age 15, a boy was sent into the forest to prepare for manhood. Men of the village beat him and tormented him, to make him strong. When he finally returned to his village, he was expected to take on a man's responsibilities. He was not allowed to even show that he remembered his former life with his mother and sisters.

Girls and women did many kinds of work in the village. They were busy all day, cooking, sewing, and caring for small children. It was the women who built houses and tended crops, although men helped them clear the fields. Girls usually married when they were 13 or 14 years old. Like the boys, they took on adult responsibilities at this age.

FAQ

Q8 WHY DID POWHATAN MEN SHAVE HALF THEIR HEADS?

A8 Men shaved the right side of their heads to keep their hair from getting in the way when they used the bow and arrow.

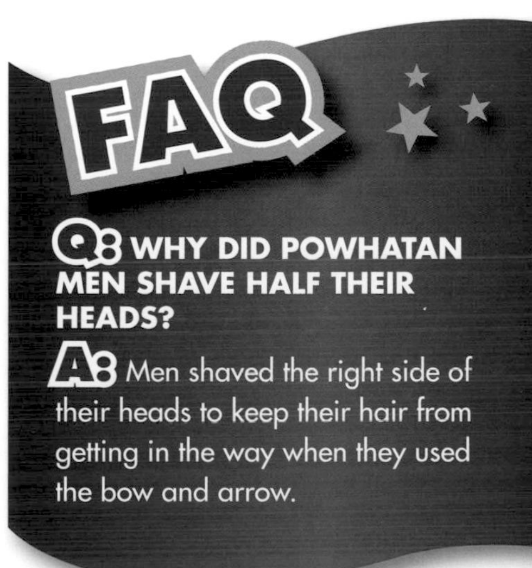

A Powhatan group sits around a fire as they pray and shake rattles.

DANCING AND HAVING FUN

At work, men and women usually lived separate lives. But when it came to dancing and playing games, everyone in the village took part. Dances were held to welcome visitors, to celebrate weddings, or just for fun. The dancers formed a circle, with one or more people stationed at the center. Drummers made the music, or someone might play a wooden flute.

Some Powhatan games were played only by men. In one, a player tried to hit a leather ball with a stick so that it flew between two upright poles. A game like football was played between teams of women and boys. Everyone enjoyed a game much like pickup sticks. Someone dropped a handful of twigs on the ground. Players tried to pick them up one by one, without disturbing the rest.

THE WORLD OF THE GODS

What made the thunder roll and the rain fall? Why did people get sick? To Powhatans, the answer was clear.

The gods caused good fortune and bad. Gods were moody and unpredictable. The most powerful of these was Okeus. If he was happy, Okeus brought health, game, and plentiful harvests. If Okeus was angry, he sent sickness, drought, and hunger.

In most Powhatan towns, one house was set aside as a temple. In the temple, priests held ceremonies to Okeus and the other gods. They gave the gods gifts of food and sang songs in their honor.

In times of trouble, people asked the priests to help win the gods' favor. The priests led dances to ask for rain or victory in battle. They also invented methods for healing the sick. Priests gathered herbs with medicinal qualities. They knew how to treat bleeding, fevers, and many infections.

In the evenings, Powhatans sat around the fire telling stories. They told of hunts and wars and long journeys by canoe. One tale described a group of pale-skinned strangers who once sailed up Chesapeake Bay in three great canoes with wings flying above them. For a few months, these strangers lived on an island in one of the rivers that flowed inland from the bay. Then they sailed away again, as mysteriously as they came. Powhatans wondered who the people were and where they had come from. They could not have imagined the changes that lay ahead when more strangers reached their land from over the sea.

Picture Yourself . . .

as a Powhatan Child

You are lying on a mat on the sleeping bench in your family's house. Your hand is swollen and sore from a bad scratch by a bramble. You feel feverish and weak. Your mother calls in the priest to see you. He squats beside you and chants for a long time, using words you can't understand. Then he rises slowly and walks back and forth, shaking a rattle above you. Finally, he hands you a bowl of steaming tea. You don't like the smell, but your mother gives you a look that means you better drink every drop! The tea has a bitter taste, but somehow you swallow it all. Soon the priest's songs carry you off to sleep. When you wake up, your fever is gone and your hand doesn't hurt anymore. The priest is gone, too. Your mother tells you to run and take him a freshly caught rabbit as a thank-you gift. Off you go, joyful to be well again.

READ ABOUT

The landing at Jamestown in 1607

1607
The first permanent English colony in North America is established at Jamestown

1619
Separate ships carrying British women and enslaved Africans arrived at Jamestown

1776 ▲
Thomas Jefferson serves as the main author of the Declaration of Independence

EXPLORATION AND SETTLEMENT

★

IN MAY 1607, AFTER 18 GRUELING WEEKS AT SEA, 105 ENGLISHMEN ABOARD THREE SHIPS SAILED UP CHESAPEAKE BAY. Some were tradesmen—carpenters, blacksmiths, or barbers. About half were gentlemen who had never worked a day in their lives. All hoped to make their fortunes in the Americas. So did the group of London businessmen who paid for the trip, an organization called the Virginia Company.

1781
The Battle of Yorktown brings an end to the American Revolution

1788 ▲
Virginia is the 10th state to ratify the U.S. Constitution

1789
Virginian George Washington becomes the first U.S. president

European Exploration of Virginia

The colored arrows on this map show the route taken by John Smith in 1608.

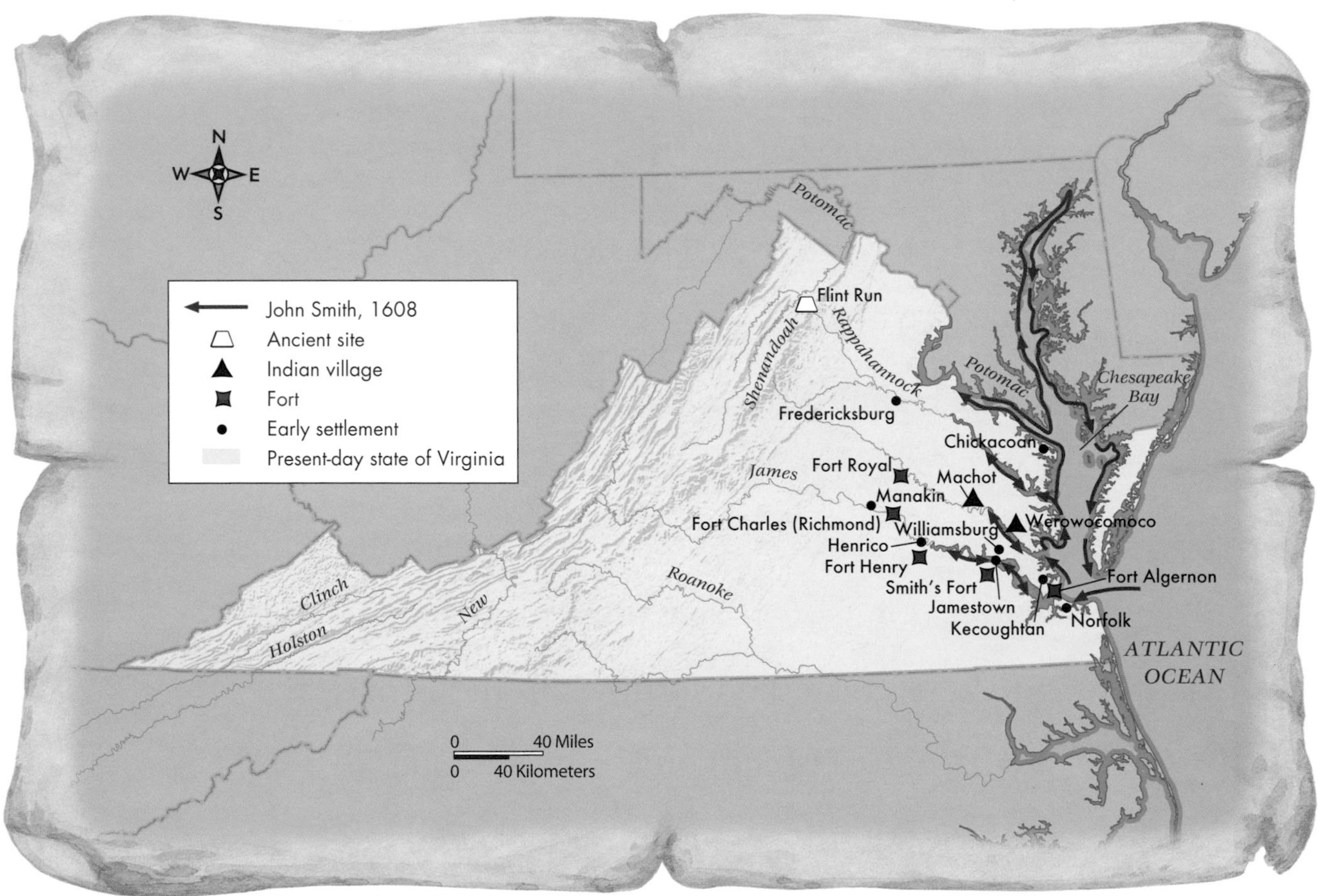

THE COLONY AT JAMESTOWN

The leader of the colonists was a brash young man named John Smith. Soon after the colonists arrived at Jamestown, Native Americans captured him and took him to their leader, Chief Powhatan. The chief put Smith through a series of tests to prove his bravery.

Pocahontas, the chief's 11-year-old daughter, was watching. Smith later claimed that Pocahontas begged her father to spare his life. He was freed and allowed to return to his men. Smith gave several different versions of this story, and no one knows for sure what really happened. But the Powhatans did welcome the English settlers, providing them with corn and bread.

The Virginia colonists built a triangular **stockade** around a church and a cluster of houses. Each of the houses had room for about a dozen people to sleep. The colonists built houses by lashing reed mats over frames they built with saplings. They raised their beds off the floor on posts. Indoor fires kept insects away and provided warmth, but the settlers were barely comfortable.

The English newcomers called their tiny settlement Jamestown, after King James I of England. It was the first permanent English settlement in North America.

Most of the Virginia colonists spent their days tramping through the woods in search of gold. They didn't know how to hunt or raise crops, and they didn't want to learn. When they struck it rich, they thought, they wouldn't need to know about such things! Smith knew that the colony would be in deep trou-

RESISTING THE SPANIARDS

Don Luis de Velasco was one of the first Native Americans to see Europe. In 1566, a Spanish ship landed on Virginia's coast. The Spanish explorers persuaded Luis de Velasco's father, an American Indian chief, to let them take his son with them back to Spain, promising that the teenager would return with great wealth. The boy learned to speak Spanish, became a Roman Catholic, and took a Spanish name. After 10 years, Spanish missionaries returned Luis de Velasco to his homeland, hoping that he would convert his people to the Catholic faith. Instead, he led an Indian uprising against the Spaniards, who fled Virginia.

WORD TO KNOW

stockade *a fort built with walls of poles driven into the ground*

Jamestown settler making bricks

MINI-BIO

JOHN SMITH: CAPTAIN AND ADVENTURER

In his early 20s, John Smith (1580–1631) traveled all over Europe and the Middle East. He was even captured in Turkey and sold into slavery! He escaped and made his way back to England. He spent two years in Virginia as leader of the Jamestown Colony. Back in England, he wrote several books about his experiences.

Want to know more? See www.apva.org/history/jsmith.html

ble unless people planted crops. It made him angry to see men idle in the summer. What were they going to do when winter came and there was no food? Smith announced a strict rule: "He who does not work, does not eat!" Only sick people were excused.

The men grumbled about Smith's rule, but they worked as he ordered. Even the gentlemen got calluses on their hands from digging and hoeing! Jamestown survived its first and second years.

In 1609, Smith had to return to England. Without his leadership, the men slipped back into their lazy ways. One eyewitness said they enjoyed "bowling in the streets." Their food supplies ran low and finally disappeared. By now, it was winter, and game was scarce. The colonists entered a desperate period they called the "starving time." They begged the Native peoples for food. The colonists knew nothing about surviving in the woods. One colonist wrote that an American Indian commented, "We can plant anywhere, and we know that you cannot live [without] our harvest."

What must Powhatans have thought of these men? They had guns—powerful weapons for hunting and warfare. Yet they knew almost nothing about diplomacy. In 1609, Chief Powhatan had confronted Smith with three questions: "Why will you take by force what you may obtain by love? Why will you destroy us who supply you with food? What can you get by war?"

Jamestown settlers trading with Native Americans in 1609

During the starving time, many colonists died of hunger and disease. At last, only 60 remained. The survivors left the fort and set off down the James, determined to go back to England. Just as they reached the harbor at present-day Hampton Roads, two English ships sailed into view! They were loaded with supplies, a new governor, and a crowd of hopeful new colonists.

Over the next few years, the fortunes of the Jamestown colonists improved. They found a source of income from a crop that the Native Americans had introduced to them: tobacco. Tobacco grew well in the marshy soil around Jamestown. Cargo ships carried dried tobacco leaves to eager buyers of the fashionable new product in London.

Planting, tending, and harvesting tobacco required many hands. As the tobacco trade grew, the English enslaved more and more Native peoples, forcing them to work in the fields.

For the first dozen years, only a handful of English women ventured to the Virginia colony. In 1619, the Virginia Company sent 90 young women to become wives for the colonists. Some of the women had been in prison and were sent against their will. Others chose to go in the hope of escaping desperate poverty.

The House of Burgesses was the world's first democratic governing body since ancient times.

HUMANS FOR SALE

In 1619, 22 English property owners formed a lawmaking body called the House of Burgesses to govern the colony along with a council that the Virginia Company appointed. The all-English House of Burgesses had hardly assembled when six Polish workmen marched on them to demand their right to vote and choose representatives as well. After a vigorous argument, the Poles were granted equal rights with the Englishmen.

In 1619, a ship carrying 20 African people arrived in Jamestown. This marked the beginning of slavery in the American colonies.

The House of Burgesses was a big step toward **democracy**. But in the same year, Virginia took a giant step backward, away from liberty and justice, when a Dutch ship arrived and anchored at Jamestown, carrying a cargo of 20 Africans. The captain explained that his supplies were running low. He offered the Africans to the colonists as **indentured servants** in exchange for corn, salt pork, and other food. The colonists agreed, and freed the Africans after some years of service.

But the idea of forcing blacks to work for no money had taken hold. In 1638, the colony's first slave auction was held, and by 1662 a law was passed that any child born to an enslaved mother was also a slave, even if the child's father was a free man.

AMERICAN INDIAN RESISTANCE

As more and more Europeans poured onto their land, Powhatans grew alarmed. At times, they tried to make peace with the newcomers and hoped to be left alone. But peace never lasted for long. Sooner or later a promise was broken, a shot was fired, and fighting flared up.

In 1622, a Powhatan chief named Opechancanough led a band of warriors against the settlements on the James River. The Powhatans caught the English by surprise and killed some 350 settlers. It was a setback for the colonists, but it didn't stop the flow of Europeans.

The Native Americans soon found that the newcomers bore secret weapons even more powerful than firearms. They brought deadly diseases that had never existed in North America before. The Native people had no **immunity** against these European sicknesses. Epidemics of measles, smallpox, and other diseases wiped out entire villages.

WORDS TO KNOW

democracy *government in which people choose their leaders*

indentured servants *people who work for others under contract*

immunity *natural protection against disease*

Africans and Indians weren't the only groups to suffer from the demand for labor. In 1619, 100 boys from London were shipped as indentured servants to Jamestown to help meet the labor shortage.

CRIMES AND PUNISHMENTS

By 1640, the government established "slave codes" to control enslaved people. In one court ruling that year, an enslaved man named Emanuel was found guilty of trying to escape. He was sentenced to receive 30 lashes and to be branded on the cheek with the letter R for "runaway." Running away to live with the Indians could be punished by hanging. Still, many enslaved Africans risked their lives to find freedom and protection in Indian villages.

The Indians of Virginia steadily lost ground. The English pushed farther inland, and the Native peoples retreated into the mountains. The once-powerful Powhatans became scattered and weakened by warfare and disease.

GROWTH OF THE COLONY

By the mid-1600s, English settlements spread along the James and York rivers all the way to the Fall Line. A network of trails and twisting roads connected outlying villages. Tobacco plantations flourished in the Tidewater. European ships loaded with supplies and goods sailed up and down Chesapeake Bay. In the Great Dismal Swamp between Virginia and North Carolina, dozens of families of color set up a farming society of their own. In the refuge of the swamp, they raised sheep, pigs, turkeys, and cows.

Children from poor families seldom attended school in colonial Virginia. But a few free schools pioneered the idea that learning is for everyone. The Syms Free School in Hampton opened its doors in 1635. It was

PAMUNKEY DIPLOMAT

Queen Anne (1650?–1725) was the name the British gave to the brilliant diplomat who ruled the Pamunkey nation between 1706 and 1725. British surveyors had cheated Pamunkeys out of their land, and the royal governor had imposed heavy taxes. Using her diplomatic skills, Queen Anne suggested leasing agreements and banned Pamunkey land sales. She and the British governor agreed that he would end his taxes if she would send her son to the College of William and Mary.

Settlers fighting Native Americans for land in 1676

The College of William and Mary was founded in 1693.

the first free school in the United States. Sometimes several families pooled their resources to start a school for their children. Each family paid a fee to cover the costs. These schools were called "old field schools" because they stood in abandoned fields.

In 1698, a fire destroyed the statehouse in Jamestown. The House of Burgesses voted to move the colony's capital to Middle Plantation, 5 miles (8 km) up the James. Middle Plantation was later renamed Williamsburg, in honor of England's king, William III.

The founders of Williamsburg dreamed of building a great city. Williamsburg had long straight streets lined with shops. Its governor's palace was one of the finest buildings in North America. The town even had a college, the College of William and Mary.

The first colonists at Jamestown had hoped to strike it rich in the Americas. Tobacco proved to be Virginia's gold. The

SEE IT HERE!

THE COLLEGE OF WILLIAM AND MARY

If you visit the College of William and Mary, you will see students hurrying to classes, toting laptops, and talking on cell phones. It may be hard to believe that students have been studying here for more than 300 years! The college's Wren Building is the oldest classroom building in the United States still in use. The President's House has been home to every college president since the school opened.

FALSE CLAIMS

In the 1600s, people thought that tobacco was a cure for many illnesses. An advertisement for Virginia tobacco read:

> Life is a smoke!—If this be true
> Tobacco will thy life renew;
> Then fear not death, nor killing care
> Whilst we have best Virginia here.

colony shipped 2,300 pounds (1,043 kilograms) of tobacco in 1616. By 1640, Virginia's tobacco exports had soared to 1.5 million pounds (680,000 kg) annually. Tobacco planters in the Tidewater lived in wealth and luxury. They enjoyed elegant balls and foxhunts, while enslaved Africans toiled to support the plantation owners' lavish lifestyles.

Life was very different for Virginians in the Piedmont and mountain regions. The land was less productive, and farms were smaller. During the late 1600s and early 1700s, slave labor did not play as major a part in the economy there as it did in the eastern regions, though this would change during the following century.

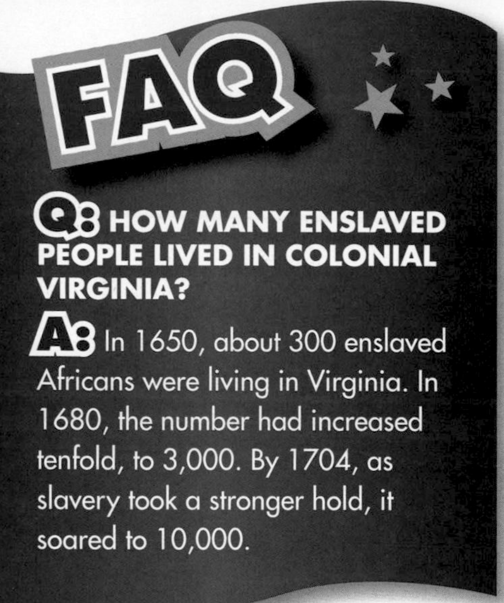

THE SEEDS OF REVOLUTION

Virginia was the first British colony in North America, but others soon formed. In the 1700s, a string of 13 English colonies stretched along the Atlantic Coast from New Hampshire to Georgia. In Virginia, the General Assembly, which included the House of Burgesses, handled most of the colony's business. But **Parliament** in London had the power to tax all of the colonies. Because they had no representatives in Parliament, many colonists thought this was not fair.

In 1773, people in Boston, Massachusetts, dumped chests of tea into Boston Harbor rather than pay tax on it. As punishment, Britain sent warships to blockade Boston Harbor. News of the punishment outraged Virginians. The House of Burgesses urged all of the 13 colonies to unite; by working together, they could demand better treatment. The First Continental Congress met in Philadelphia, Pennsylvania, in the summer of 1774. The Second Continental Congress met the following summer.

WORD TO KNOW

Parliament *a governing body in certain countries (such as Great Britain), similar to the U.S. Congress*

King George III and the British Parliament were stubborn. Instead of bargaining with the colonists, they sent troops to keep them in line. In March 1775, a Virginian named Patrick Henry gave a fiery speech in the House of Burgesses. "The war has actually begun!" he declared. "Is life so dear or peace so sweet as to be purchased at the price of chains and slavery? . . . I know not what course others may take, but as for me, give me liberty or give me death!"

The colonists and the British fought the first battle of the American Revolution in Massachusetts in April 1775. The Continental Congress appointed a Virginian named George Washington to serve as commander in chief of the Continental army. He was

Picture Yourself . . .

at the Dawn of the American Revolution

It's late at night, but you hear voices from the drawing room. Your father is talking to your uncle, who rode in this afternoon with news from Williamsburg. Their voices are loud and excited. You don't understand all their talk about stamps and taxes, but you know they are angry.

You slip out of bed and tiptoe to the top of the stairs. "Next thing you know, they'll be taxing our tobacco!" your uncle says. "Where will it end?"

"It could end in war," your father says, and his voice sounds sad. "War with the British." His words echo in your head. How could the people of Virginia fight against the king? It doesn't seem possible, but your father has uttered the dreadful word "war!"

George Washington (on horseback) leading the Continental army during a battle at Princeton, New Jersey

MINI-BIO

GEORGE WASHINGTON: THE FATHER OF OUR COUNTRY

Born in Westmoreland County, George Washington (1732–1799) enjoyed a life of wealth and privilege. As a young man, he worked mapping land on the frontier. He was a member of the House of Burgesses from 1759 to 1774. During the American Revolution, he served as a delegate to the Continental Congress and commander in chief of the Continental army. After the war, he served two terms as the first president of the United States (1789–1797). For his heroic leadership during the Revolution, in the United States he is called the Father of Our Country.

Want to know more? See www.whitehouse.gov/history/presidents/gw1.html

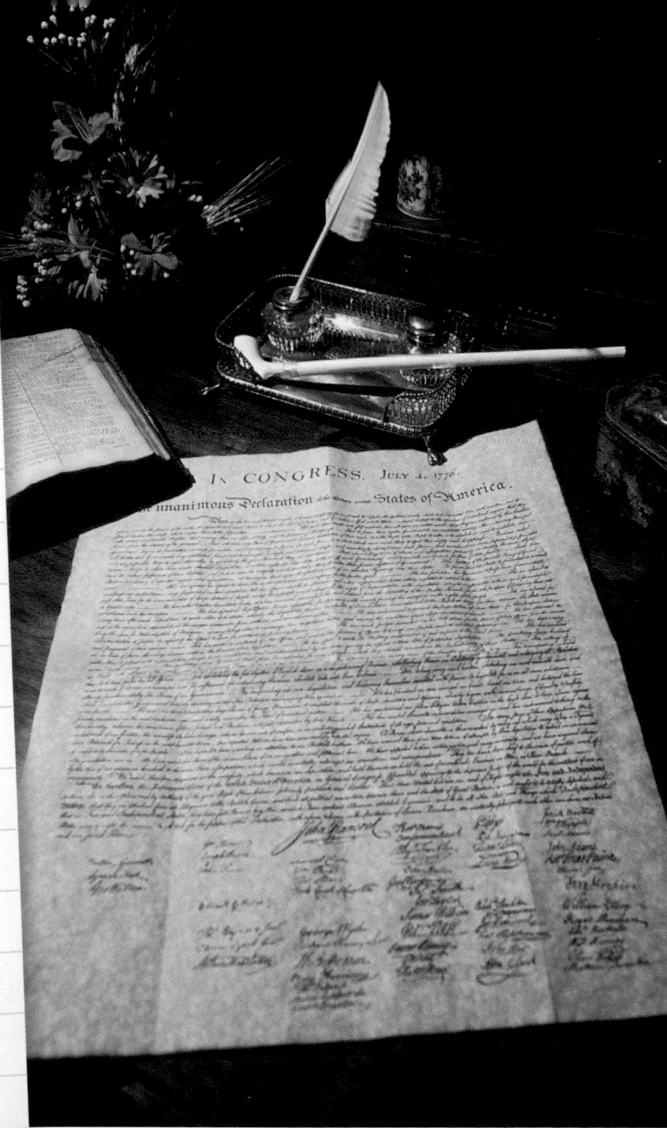

This is a copy of the Declaration of Independence, which was adopted in 1776. The Declaration was signed by a group of men who were willing to challenge the British government.

Thomas Jefferson denounced slavery in the first draft of the Declaration of Independence but deleted this statement when delegates from two slaveholding colonies objected.

selected in large part because of his political influence in Virginia, a colony that the Congress wanted to ensure would participate in the war. Under Washington's leadership, a collection of farmers and frontiersmen became a fighting force, ready to defy Europe's best troops.

As the conflict heated up, many colonists demanded a complete break from the mother country. Virginian Thomas Jefferson drafted a fiery Declaration of Independence that championed severing all ties to

England. On July 4, 1776, delegates to the Continental Congress from all 13 colonies voted to adopt it, though it took several more years of war to achieve this break.

THE FINAL BATTLE

Most of the American Revolution was fought in the northern colonies. Toward the end of the war, however, the action moved south. In June 1781, British general Charles Cornwallis gathered nearly 10,000 troops at the Virginia port of Yorktown. From this base, he hoped to subdue the southern colonies. With 20,000 troops, Washington surrounded the British force. For weeks, Washington held Yorktown under siege. France aided the battle by providing American patriots with money and munitions, which played a pivotal role in ending the war. At last, after a long and bloody battle, Cornwallis surrendered. Virginia and the other colonies had won the war!

MINI-BIO

THOMAS JEFFERSON: A MAN OF MANY TALENTS

Thomas Jefferson (1743–1826) was the lead author of the Declaration of Independence and third president of the United States. He also deeply valued education and ideas. He studied ancient tools and bones, explored better ways to grow tobacco and other crops, and read the works of European philosophers. Toward the end of his life, he poured his energy into starting a university. He designed the buildings, chose the courses, and picked the teachers. He even donated all the books from his personal library! The University of Virginia, Jefferson's gift to his native state, opened in 1825.

Want to know more? See www.monticello.org/jefferson/biography.html

The surrender of General Cornwallis (center standing) after the Battle of Yorktown

Virginia: From Territory to Statehood

(1609–1788)

This map shows the original Virginia territory and the area (outlined in green) that became the commonwealth of Virginia in 1788.

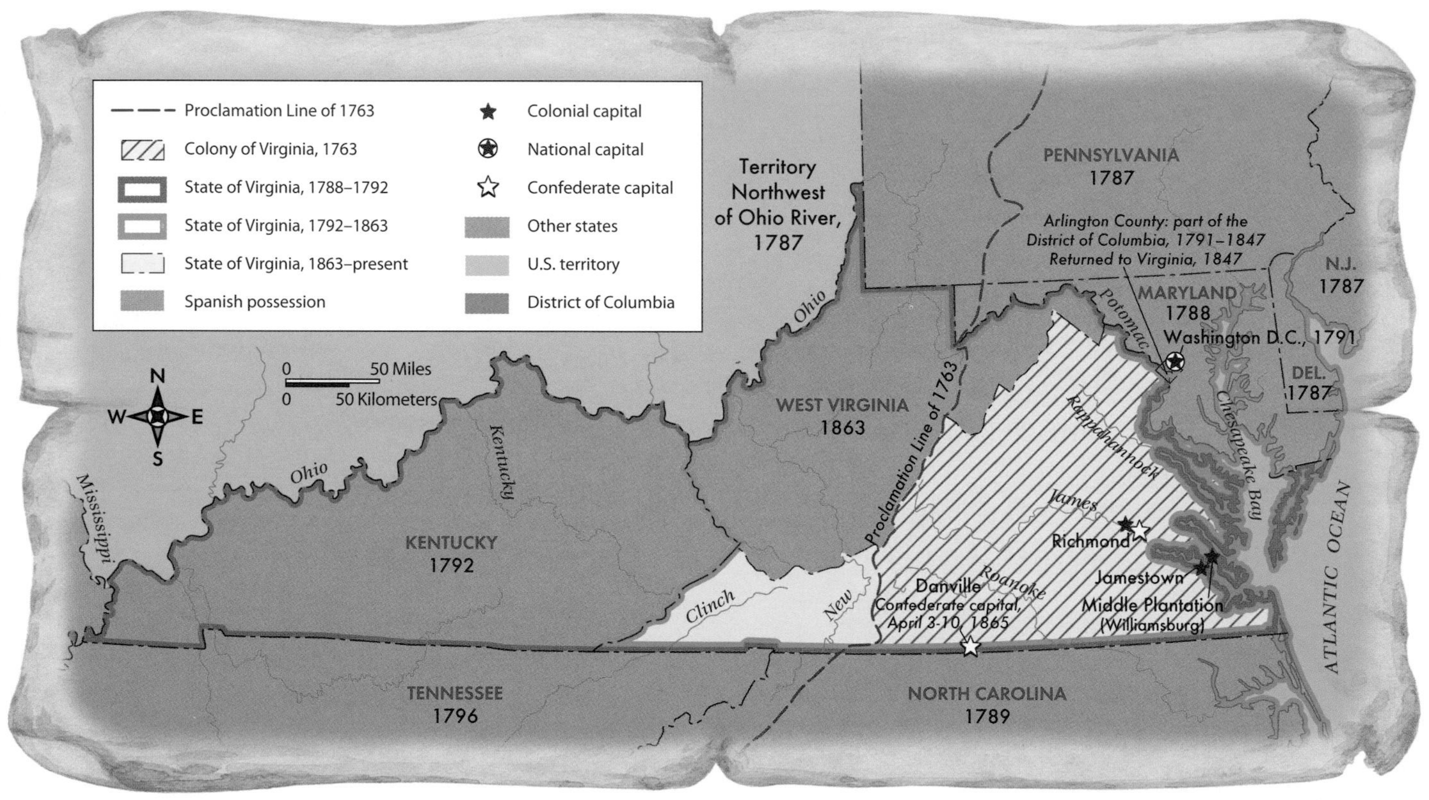

NEW LAWS FOR A NEW NATION

How was the new nation to be governed? Most people felt loyal to the state where they lived. They thought of themselves as Pennsylvanians or Virginians, rather than Americans. The Continental Congress created a set of governing laws called the Articles of Confederation. All of the states had to ratify, or approve, these laws.

But Maryland was afraid that its neighbor, Virginia, was too strong and powerful. Virginia had the highest population of any of the states and by far the most territory—as a colony, it included the present-day states of Ohio, Indiana, Illinois, Michigan, and Wisconsin. Finally, Virginia agreed to give up these western lands. Under the Articles of Confederation, the bonds among the states were loose and uncertain.

Some leaders, including Virginian James Madison, believed the United States should have a strong central government. He was concerned that people would act on their self-interests, so he proposed a government with strong branches that shared power and could balance the opposing interests of the individuals in each branch. In the summer of 1787, a convention met in Philadelphia to design a new **constitution**. Madison largely created the document. It offered a Congress with two houses. All of the states would have equal representation in the upper house, or Senate. In the lower house, or House of Representatives, the number of representatives depended on the state's voting population.

After much debate, Virginia's delegates to the Constitutional Convention signed the document. On June 25, 1788, Virginia became the 10th state to join the United States of America.

WORD TO KNOW

constitution *a written document that contains all the governing principles of a state or country*

The signing of the U.S. Constitution in 1787

READ ABOUT

A slave auction in Virginia, 1861

1800
Gabriel Prosser's plans for a slave revolt are discovered

1859 ▲
John Brown leads a rebellion at Harpers Ferry

1861
Virginia secedes from the Union

GROWTH AND CHANGE

★

AS THE YOUNG NATION TOOK ITS FIRST STEPS FORWARD, VIRGINIA CONTINUED TO PRODUCE ITS MAJOR LEADERS. Four of the first five U.S. presidents were Virginians. But the issue of slavery still haunted Virginia. How could freedom and enslavement exist side by side?

1862

The Monitor *and the* Merrimac *clash near Hampton Roads harbor*

1865 ►

Robert E. Lee surrenders at Appomattox Court House

1870

Virginia returns to the Union with a new constitution

Enslaved people worked long days on Virginia cotton plantations.

A STATE DIVIDED

In 1800, farmers in the Tidewater were worried. The soil was worn out from growing tobacco year after year. A planter couldn't make a good living anymore. Some Tidewater planters were already experimenting with new crops. Cotton flourished on soil that no longer had the minerals tobacco required. But it was time-consuming and tedious to remove seeds from raw cotton fibers. Enslaved workers tended the cotton plants and processed the cotton bolls by hand.

In 1793, a new invention called the cotton engine, or cotton gin, made cleaning cotton bolls easier and less expensive. But it didn't improve life for African Americans at all; with the cotton gin, slavery skyrocketed in Virginia.

Between the Tidewater and the west lay a widening gap. The Tidewater planters tended to look down on the western farmers as rough and ignorant. The western farmers planted fields with cotton, wheat, and corn. Some raised sheep and hogs. They often resented the Tidewater planters, who were rich in power, money, and slaves and didn't have to worry about American Indian raids. Besides wanting a greater voice in government, the westerners wanted the state to protect their scattered settlements from such attacks. In 1780, the capital of Virginia was moved from Williamsburg to the town of Richmond on the Piedmont. But it didn't help the western cause. People in the Tidewater still thought the mountain farmers should defend themselves.

PLANTATION LIFE

Large tobacco or cotton plantations were self-sufficient. Their gardens and henhouses produced enough food for enslaved workers and for the family in the "big house." Most clothing was made on the plantation.

Plantation owners often filled their homes with fine furniture imported from Europe. The planters and their families lived cultured lives. They read widely and wore elegant clothes. They threw grand parties and dinners. Virginians such as Dolley Madison, wife of future president James Madison, prided themselves on being warm and gracious hosts. The planters' children were

MINI-BIO

DOLLEY MADISON: BELOVED FIRST LADY

Dolley Madison (1768–1849) was born in North Carolina to a family from Virginia. In 1794, she married James Madison. After Madison became U.S. secretary of state in 1801, Dolley became the most important woman in Washington society. She was warm, fashionable, and welcoming, the ideal Virginia host. When James Madison became president, Dolley created the role of a public "first lady," charming visiting officials and American citizens alike.

Want to know more? See www.whitehouse.gov/history/firstladies/dm4.html

While many plantation owners lived in huge mansions, enslaved workers had cabins like these.

tutored at home. Boys learned Greek, Latin, science, and mathematics. Girls were taught to draw, sew, and play a musical instrument.

While planter families enjoyed lives of ease and luxury, enslaved workers tended the crops, scrubbed the floors, cooked the meals, and cared for the children. Slave owners were often cruel. One Virginia man recalled his grandmother's stories of her life as a slave: "Grandma said slaves had to pick so many pounds of cotton a day, and they were given an awful whipping if they didn't get this amount. . . . All the slaves who had fallen short had to stand in line with their backs bare for their whipping." Worst of all, a slave could be bought or sold like a horse or a piece of furniture—and forced to leave family and friends.

Slave owners lived with a constant, simmering fear. Surrounded by people who had every reason to hate them, they never felt safe. In 1800, a young enslaved man named Gabriel Prosser made careful plans for an uprising in Richmond. Prosser gathered weapons and mobilized up to 1,000 African Americans, enslaved and free. But his plot was discovered. His captains were arrested and hanged. Governor James Monroe, fearing the entire countryside was about to rise up against slavery, called on U.S. armed forces to crush a slave rebellion. The Virginia legislature held secret sessions to discuss ending slavery. In 1808, the U.S. Congress, fearful of violence, outlawed the slave trade.

As the years passed, white Virginians tightened control over enslaved people. Then, in 1831, an enslaved preacher named Nat Turner organized a band of 40 to 60 men who marched toward the village of Cross Keys in Southampton County and its storehouse of ammunition. The group spared a poor white family but killed more than four dozen slaveholders and their families. U.S. troops and naval vessels rushed to surround Turner's band. Turner surrendered and was executed. He became a folk hero to African Americans. Soon after, the Virginia legislature vigorously debated whether to end slavery or tighten slave restrictions. Stricter slave codes were passed.

It took cleverness and courage to escape slavery. In 1848, Henry Brown climbed into a box in Richmond, and a white friend mailed him by express to Philadelphia.

THE CALL FOR ABOLITION

How could a country that believed in freedom and equality also allow slavery? In the first part of the 19th century, people struggled with this question. The Northern states passed laws that gradually brought slavery to an end. Slavery remained woven into the fabric of life in Virginia and other Southern states.

Many people in the North argued that slavery should be ended completely, or abolished. Known as **abolitionists**, they sought to keep slavery from spreading into new

WORD TO KNOW

abolitionists *people who were opposed to slavery and worked to end it*

John Brown and his group holding hostages at an engine house at Harpers Ferry

states that joined the growing nation. Many also helped runaway slaves escape to freedom in the North. Many white Virginians, such as Patrick Henry, believed that slavery was wrong. However, most claimed it was a necessary evil. Virginians feared that without slave labor, their economy would collapse.

In 1859, an abolitionist named John Brown organized an uprising at Harpers Ferry, Virginia (in present-day West Virginia). Brown led 19 men, including five African Americans and some of his own sons, to seize a federal arsenal. He hoped to free a group of enslaved people, lead them into the mountains, and from there launch raids that would bring down the system. Captured and executed, Brown was denounced by slaveholders and glorified by Northern authors and abolitionists. Less than two years after his death, U.S. soldiers marched into battle singing, "John Brown's body lies a-moldering in the grave, but his truth goes marching on."

INTO WAR

In November 1860, Abraham Lincoln was elected president of the United States. Lincoln was determined that slavery should not spread to new territories and states. He did not, however, intend to free the slaves in states where slavery was already established.

Almost as soon as Lincoln was elected, South Carolina seceded, or broke away, from the United States. South Carolina planters were afraid that Lincoln would free all slaves. Six more Southern states quickly followed South Carolina's lead. Together, these seven states formed a new nation, the Confederate States of America.

In early 1861, Virginians voted against seceding, but the issue divided much of the population. Then, on April 12, 1861, Confederate troops opened fire on Fort Sumter in the harbor of Charleston, South Carolina. Fort Sumter was a U.S. Army fort, but now Confederates claimed it was on their soil. After two days, the federal troops at the fort surrendered. The Civil War had begun.

Three days after Fort Sumter surrendered, Virginia seceded from the Union. Because Virginia was such a powerful state, it became the backbone of

MINI-BIO

MARY PEAKE: FREEDOM FIGHTER

Mary Peake (1823–1862) was born free in Norfolk and educated in a private school for African Americans in Alexandria. When she completed her schooling, she taught enslaved children in Norfolk, working in secret because it was illegal to teach slaves to read and write. When the Civil War broke out, she and her family took refuge at Union-held Fort Monroe near Hampton. During the war's first year, she taught black children and gave night classes for black adults. She died at the age of 39.

Want to know more? See http://mac110.assumption.edu/aas/Manuscripts/marypeakeappend.html

MINI-BIO

ROBERT E. LEE: UNCLE ROBERT

Robert E. Lee (1807–1870) graduated from West Point Military Academy with an outstanding record. During the Civil War, he commanded all Confederate operations in Virginia. He quickly won the devotion of his men, who nicknamed him "Uncle Robert." He was finally defeated at Petersburg in 1865 and forced to surrender at Appomattox Court House. After the war, Lee served as president of Washington College (now called Washington and Lee University) until his death.

Want to know more? See www.nps.gov/arho/historyculture/robert-lee.htm

the Confederacy. Confederate president Jefferson Davis lived and worked in Richmond, the Confederate capital, until the end of the war.

Not all Virginians favored secession. U.S. Army colonel Robert E. Lee was a Virginian whose loyalties were torn between his state and his country. When President Lincoln asked him to command the Union army, Lee struggled with his decision. At last he decided, "I cannot raise my hand against my birthplace, my home, my children." Lee instead became a Confederate, serving as the commander of the Army of Northern Virginia.

Q: WHY DO THE SAME CIVIL WAR BATTLES HAVE DIFFERENT NAMES?

A: Southerners called the fight at Manassas the First Battle of Manassas, but Northerners called it the First Battle of Bull Run. That's because Southerners usually named battles after the nearest town, while Northerners named battles after the nearest body of water.

YEARS OF BLOODSHED

At first, most Americans thought the war would last only a few weeks. On July 21, 1861, a crowd of Northerners and Southerners gathered to watch an encounter between Union and Confederate forces at Manassas, Virginia. People brought baskets of food and settled down to enjoy an afternoon picnic, as if they were attending a football game and rooting for their favorite team. To their horror, guns roared, horses screamed and stampeded, and men suffered terrible wounds. Four thousand men lost their lives. The Confederates drove the Union forces back, but it was clear the war would not end soon.

Union and Confederate soldiers at the Battle of Spotsylvania in May 1864

Virginians marched proudly into war, eager to uphold their state's honor. But the war brought Virginia bloodshed, destruction, and grief. Virginia was the site of more than 2,200 battles, more than half of all those fought in the Civil War. Soldiers raided farms for food. They burned houses, dug up fields, and stole cattle. In 1863, a Union soldier described what he saw in Stafford County: "Buildings were levelled; fences burned; . . . the feet of men, and hoofs of horses and mules trampled fields of vegetation into barren wastes; every landmark was destroyed."

The world's first battle between two ironclad warships took place on March 9, 1862, at Hampton Roads harbor. The *Monitor* (Union) and the *Merrimac* (Confederate) fired at each other all day, but their armor plating protected both ships from serious damage.

LOSING WEST VIRGINIA

The Civil War widened the rift between eastern Virginia and its northwestern counties. When Virginians voted to secede in 1861, those in the northwestern counties strongly opposed it. To remain in the Union, they wanted to form a new state. Under the U.S. Constitution, a new state couldn't be carved out of an existing state without its approval. Representatives in western Virginia created what they named a "reorganized government of Virginia" and declared Virginia's secession illegal. The U.S. government recognized this western Virginia government's authority, allowing these counties to then propose becoming a new state. Though this collection of counties didn't officially enter the Union as the state of West Virginia until June 20, 1863, they never again acted as part of Virginia after April 1861.

Members of the 107th United States Colored Troops stand outside a guardhouse at Fort Corcoran.

SEE IT HERE!

FREDERICKSBURG BATTLEFIELD

More than 15,000 men were killed in and around the city of Fredericksburg during four bloody Civil War battles. The area is sometimes described as the bloodiest landscape in North America. In 1863, General Robert E. Lee won crushing victories at the battles of Fredericksburg and Chancellorsville, but Union forces under General Ulysses S. Grant defeated Lee at the Wilderness and Spotsylvania a year later. Today, all four battlefields welcome visitors. Maps and videos show movements of troops. Follow in their footsteps, and imagine the roar of the cannons.

The Civil War filled enslaved African Americans with hope for freedom. Hundreds of Virginia slaves fled their plantations to join the Union army, but they were not allowed to enlist as soldiers until 1863. More than 5,000 African Americans from Virginia served in the Union army and navy. Lincoln and others first doubted they could fight against white soldiers. But nationwide, 200,000 former slaves fought in hundreds of battles and skirmishes, and 18 earned Medals of Honor for their heroism. Lincoln admitted that without them, he would have had to abandon the battlefield in three weeks. Their service was especially crucial in the Battle of Petersburg, the last major battle of the war.

MINI-BIO

THOMAS "STONEWALL" JACKSON: A WALL OF STONE

A longtime resident of Lexington, Thomas Jonathan Jackson (1824–1863) became a legendary general of the Confederacy. He was so unshakable that in the midst of battle, General Barnard Bee called him a stone wall, thus earning him his nickname. The general was accidentally shot and killed by a Confederate sentry as he returned to his encampment.

Want to know more?
See www.nps.gov/frsp/js.htm

Petersburg fell to Union forces on April 1, 1865, and with it, the North took control of Richmond. Forty hours after Confederate president Jefferson Davis fled Richmond, black cavalrymen escorted Lincoln as he walked the city's streets. Former slaves greeted the president with shouts of joy. At last, on April 9, 1865, Robert E. Lee surrendered at the Virginia town of Appomattox Court House. The terms of the surrender, written by Union general Ulysses S. Grant and based on Lincoln's plan for restoring the Union, pardoned most of Lee's troops. It allowed them to return to their homes without punishment after pledging their support to the United States. The Civil War was over. It had lasted almost exactly four years. Healing from this terrible conflict would take more than a century.

TRAGEDY AND RECONSTRUCTION

After the war, the South was in ruins. Northerners and Southerners felt bitter toward each other, and neither side trusted the other. Millions of newly freed slaves had to rebuild their lives with no possessions and no education. Lincoln knew that both he and the nation faced an enormous amount of work. For starters, he needed to restore the Confederate states peacefully to the Union.

Then, on the night of April 14, 1865, Lincoln and his wife attended a play at Ford's Theatre in Washington. Out of the shadows, an actor named John Wilkes Booth shot the president in the back of the head. Booth leaped

John Wilkes Booth

onto the stage and shouted the Virginia state motto, "*Sic semper tyrannis*!" (Thus Always to Tyrants!). Lincoln died the following morning.

Friends helped Booth escape across the Potomac into Virginia. He hid in a tobacco barn in Port Royal until U.S. soldiers discovered his hiding place on April 25. They shot and killed Booth as he tried to flee.

The war had ended, but violence in the South was far from over. African Americans embraced freedom with joy and wonder. Some set out to hunt for lost relatives. Others stayed on their plantations to work as paid laborers. Many streamed away from the cotton fields in search of better work. But former slaveholders resented the freed African Americans and made their new lives difficult. Ex-slaves protested as free men and women. At a large meeting in Virginia, African Americans declared, "We have no means of legally making or enforcing contracts, . . . we have no right to testify before the courts in any case in which a white man is one of the parties; we are taxed without representation."

The federal Freedmen's Bureau helped African Americans find homes and jobs and opened schools for them. In 1868, the 14th Amendment to the U.S. Constitution gave full citizenship to black men. Two years later, the 15th Amendment guaranteed them the right to vote. (White and black women did not gain this right until 1920.)

But Southern whites made it difficult or impossible for African Americans to exercise this new right. It took U.S. Army troops to enforce the law. For a short time, former slaves held 16 percent of the seats in the Virginia legislature. They debated issues vigorously and "mingled freely with the other members," but the white majority ignored their ideas because they were uneducated.

A family of sharecroppers outside their Virginia home in 1899

One place where blacks could get an education was the Hampton Institute in Hampton. Other Virginia schools and colleges for African Americans were established, but most former slaves couldn't afford to attend them. They worked as **sharecroppers**, renting fields and equipment at unfair prices set by plantation owners. White planters made sharecropping so expensive that blacks and poor whites were always in debt to them.

Before Virginia could reenter the Union, it had to write and approve a new state constitution. The new constitution declared that Virginia would give African American men full voting privileges. On January 26, 1870, Virginia was readmitted to the United States.

WORD TO KNOW

sharecroppers *farmers who give a portion of their crops as rent for the land*

READ ABOUT

Representative Frank J. Ferrell (left) introduces Terence Powderly at the Knights of Labor convention in Richmond, 1886

1888 ►
John Mercer Langston becomes the first African American to serve in Congress

1917
World War I spurs Virginia's shipping industry

1944
Irene Morgan challenges segregation on public buses

MORE MODERN TIMES

★

ONCE-POWERFUL WHITE PLANTERS WERE OUTRAGED. Suddenly, the men who used to groom their horses, pick their cotton, and run their cotton gins sat in the statehouse in Richmond! When Virginia reentered the Union, planters set to work to bring back the old social order. In the 1870s, Virginia began to pass laws that called for the strict separation of the races.

1990
L. Douglas Wilder is elected the first African American governor in U.S. history

2001 ▸
Terrorists fly a hijacked plane into the Pentagon

2007
Virginia celebrates the 400th anniversary of the founding of Jamestown

A teacher reads to students at a segregated school in the town of Uno.

THE DAWN OF JIM CROW

The system of **segregation** that separated the races in Virginia was called Jim Crow. It required that schools, hospitals, and all other facilities be separate but equal. Equality was rarely the case, however. Schools for black children had fewer books and teachers than those for whites, and the teachers were paid much less than teachers of white children. On trains, the cars reserved for black passengers were closest to the engine. They were noisy and full of smoke. Whites rode farther back, in cars that were quiet and clean. By 1900, Jim Crow laws were in place throughout the American South.

WORD TO KNOW

segregation *separation from others, according to race, class, ethnic group, religion, or other factors*

In the early 1880s, a small association of white and black reformers, known as the Readjusters, gained some political force. The Readjusters united with the minority political party, and together they were able to gain control of the state government. They increased aid for public schools for both races, ended the **poll tax** that kept poor people from voting, and put a stop to whipping poor prisoners of both races. But the Readjusters were soon driven from power.

In 1888, John Mercer Langston became Virginia's first black representative to the U.S. Congress. But in 1902, Virginia's legislature feared that poor blacks and poor whites might unite, so it passed laws to prevent this from happening. A new poll tax was passed, and

WORD TO KNOW

poll tax *a fee that people must pay before they can vote*

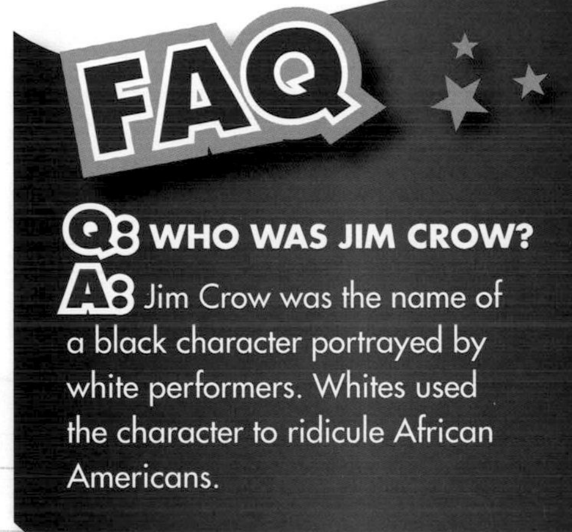

Q: WHO WAS JIM CROW?

A: Jim Crow was the name of a black character portrayed by white performers. Whites used the character to ridicule African Americans.

MINI-BIO

JOHN MERCER LANGSTON: PIONEER FOR FREEDOM

John Mercer Langston (1829–1897) was born free in Louisa County. Denied entrance to law school because of his African ancestry, he studied on his own and passed the Ohio bar exam in 1854. Langston organized antislavery societies and helped runaway slaves. During the Civil War, he recruited African American soldiers for the Union army. After the war, he served as president of the Virginia Normal and Collegiate Institute. In 1888, he became the first African American to serve in Congress.

Want to know more? See www.oberlin.edu/EOG/OYTT-images/JMLangston.html

Ships dock at a pier in Norfolk where coal is loaded for transport.

a literacy test was required that could be used to disqualify people of color from voting. The fight for **civil rights** would continue well into the 20th century.

WORD TO KNOW

civil rights *basic rights that are guaranteed to all people under the U.S. Constitution*

CHANGING WAYS

Tobacco, the "gold" of colonial days, helped rescue Virginia from its Civil War debt. A new variety of tobacco, called bright-leaf, grew well in Virginia's soil. Many Virginians found jobs in tobacco-processing plants near Richmond.

Virginians found work in many other industries as well. Cotton-processing plants turned cotton bolls into soft, durable fabric. Coalfields opened in Virginia's southwestern corner. Gravel, granite, and limestone mines employed many. In cities, banking and newspaper publishing industries boomed. More and more railroads crisscrossed the state, connecting it and its products to the rest of the nation.

In 1914, World War I broke out in Europe. Virginia-born president Woodrow Wilson promised to keep the United States neutral. But he was unable to keep his word, and in 1917 the United States entered the war. The nation needed vast numbers of transport ships to carry soldiers and supplies to Europe. So war gave a push to the shipbuilding industry that was developing in Newport News.

The 1920s brought money and good times to many Virginians, but the state still had many desperately poor farming people, both black and white. In 1926, Governor Harry F. Byrd set to work tightening up the state's government. He found ways to cut down waste and save money. Virginia was finally on the road to recovery and growth.

Then in 1929, banks across the country began to fail. Factories closed, and jobless men wandered America's streets. The United States fell into a deep economic depression. As prices for crops tumbled, farmers slipped into debt. Thousands of teenagers, mostly boys, took to the road looking for work. During this time, many Virginians fared better than other Americans because Virginia's economy was based on a large variety of industries, but Virginia's poorest were hit hard.

MINI-BIO

HARRY F. BYRD: DOLLARS AND CENTS

Harry F. Byrd (1887–1966) of Berryville belonged to one of the oldest families in Virginia. From 1926 to 1930, he served as governor of the state. He entered the U.S. Senate in 1933 and served there until his death. In Virginia, he encouraged historic preservation and the building of roads. He liked to say, "When you have to hunt for them, you get to know how many cents there really are in a dollar."

Want to know more?
See www.lva.lib.va.us/whoweare/exhibits/political/harry_byrd.htm

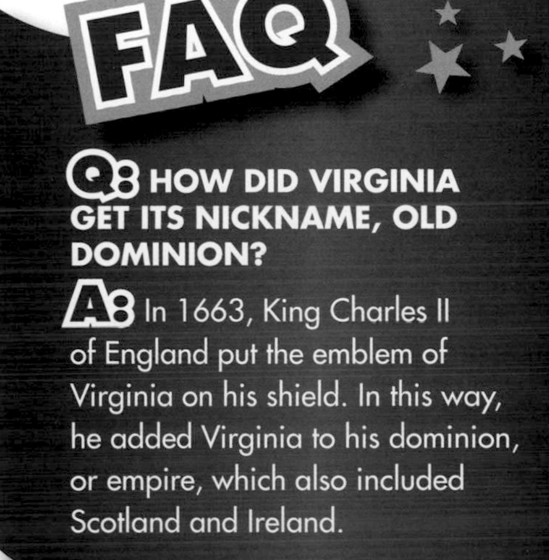

FAQ

Q8 HOW DID VIRGINIA GET ITS NICKNAME, OLD DOMINION?

A8 In 1663, King Charles II of England put the emblem of Virginia on his shield. In this way, he added Virginia to his dominion, or empire, which also included Scotland and Ireland.

SEE IT HERE!

THE PENTAGON

On January 15, 1943, a building called the Pentagon was opened in Arlington to provide temporary space for the overcrowded War Department. There was nothing temporary about it, however. Today, the Pentagon is headquarters of the U.S. Department of Defense. It is one of the biggest office buildings in the world. Its five wedge-shaped sections have three times the floor space of the Empire State Building in New York City! About 26,000 people work there every day.

VIRGINIA AT WAR

On the morning of December 7, 1941, Virginians heard stunning news. Japanese bombers had destroyed most of the U.S. naval fleet at Pearl Harbor in Hawai'i. The attack plunged the United States into World War II. The country had to rebuild its naval fleet. With its shipbuilding facilities at Norfolk and Newport News, Virginia helped restore the navy to a powerful fighting force. Preparations for the war created so much work for people throughout the United States that the Great Depression soon ended.

GROWING INDUSTRIES

With the inflow of military people and their families during World War II, Virginia's population soared. After the war, many newcomers decided to stay. Thriving suburbs blossomed around Washington, D.C. One developer, Robert E. Simon, tried to create a model community in Fairfax County called Reston. The first

A view of the Norfolk Navy Yard in Portsmouth, 1941

section of Reston opened in 1965. Simon believed that people should live in high-rise apartments surrounded by open space. This would allow plenty of room for parks and other recreation areas. Reston has many parks, as well as four human-made lakes.

In the postwar years, Virginia encouraged businesses to move to the state. Manufacturing surged, and agriculture slipped into the background.

More Virginians meant a need for better roads and bridges. In 1964, an amazing construction project was completed. The Chesapeake Bay Bridge-Tunnel opened, linking the Eastern Shore with the mainland. The Bridge-Tunnel stretches 17 miles (27 km) from Virginia Beach to the Eastern Shore. It is a series of bridges, tunnels, and human-made islands and has been called one of the Seven Wonders of the Modern World.

THE CIVIL RIGHTS MOVEMENT

One morning in 1944, Irene Morgan, a 27-year-old African American mother of two who worked making bombers for the war effort, sat on a bus. According to law and custom, blacks were required to give up their seats to whites. But Morgan refused to move. She recalled that a sheriff's deputy "put his hand on me to arrest me, so I took my foot and kicked him."

Morgan refused to pay a $10 fine for violating Virginia's segregation law, and the National Association for the Advancement of Colored People (NAACP) asked lawyers Thurgood Marshall and William Hastie to plead her case before the Supreme Court. In 1946, the high court ruled 6 to 1 in favor of Morgan that segregation on interstate buses was illegal. In 2000, Gloucester County honored her contribution to democracy. The next year, President Bill Clinton awarded her the Presidential

MINI-BIO

OLIVER W. HILL: FIGHTING FOR JUSTICE

As a young black lawyer in the 1940s, Oliver W. Hill (1907–2007) had one driving purpose. Through the courts, he wanted to fight for equality between the races. He won his first major case in 1940, gaining equal pay for black teachers in Norfolk. In the early 1950s, he worked on several school desegregation cases in Virginia. Angry whites threatened his family and burned a cross on his lawn. Hill did not back down. He practiced civil rights law for almost 60 years, finally retiring in 1998.

Want to know more? See www.pbs.org/beyondbrown/history/oliverhill.html

Citizens Medal. The citation read, "She took the first step on a journey that would change America forever." Thurgood Marshall later became an associate justice on the U.S. Supreme Court.

The ruling, however, didn't change segregation in Virginia or the rest of the South. The old Jim Crow laws remained entrenched. Whites and blacks had to use separate drinking fountains and sit in separate sections of movie theaters. The seats at the front of the bus were reserved for whites; blacks had to sit in the back. Even hospital blood supplies were separated according to whether the blood donor was black or white. Irene Morgan's brave action was one of the first skirmishes in a revolution that would sweep across the South.

In 1951, Barbara Johns, a 16-year-old African American student at the all-black R. R. Moton High School in Farmville, Virginia, was frustrated by her school's severe overcrowding and the school board's refusal to address the problem. Johns organized and staged a walkout with some 300 of her classmates in protest. Soon after, the NAACP joined the fight, filing suit for an integrated school for the students. This case was one of five similar suits that made it to the Supreme Court. In 1954, the Court made a groundbreaking decision when it ruled that "separate is not equal" in the education of black and white children. In the case of *Brown v. Board of Education*, the Court outlawed racially segregated schools throughout the country.

This elementary school in Fort Myer was integrated in 1954.

In Virginia, and across the South, schools that chose to desegregate were taken over by the state and closed. State and federal courts found these state-forced closures to be unconstitutional,. and all schools were ordered reopened.

But whites in Prince Edward County would not give in. Rather than **integrate** its schools, the county refused to budget money for education. For almost six years, from 1958 until 1964, all public schools in the county shut down. Some families sent their children to live with relatives in states where they could attend classes. Others organized small private schools. But about 1,780 children, both black and white, did not attend school at all. In 1964, the U.S. Supreme Court ordered the county to levy a tax and reopen its schools.

WORD TO KNOW

integrate *to bring together all members of society as equals*

All over Virginia, black and white children sat together in classrooms. The old "whites only" signs disappeared from restrooms and drinking fountains. Anyone could sit anywhere on any bus. Jim Crow had ended.

The end of segregation opened the way for African Americans to play a role in state and local politics. In 1967, physician and Korean War veteran William F. Reid became the first black delegate elected to the state legislature since 1891. In 1990, Virginia became the first state to choose an African American as governor, with the election of L. Douglas Wilder.

INTO THE NEXT CENTURY

Virginia entered the 21st century with a spirit of optimism. The economy was strong, and people had a sense of hope.

Tragedy struck on September 11, 2001, when terrorists crashed a plane into the Pentagon. The attack took the lives of 125 people on the ground, as well as all those aboard the flight. Two other hijacked planes destroyed the Twin Towers of the World Trade Center in New York City, and a fourth hijacked plane crashed in rural Pennsylvania, killing everyone aboard. Virginia and the nation reeled with shock. Expressions of sympathy poured in from all over the world.

The year 2007 marked the 400th anniversary of the founding of Jamestown, the first permanent English settlement in North America. Kicking off the yearlong festivities, a replica of the *Godspeed* sailed up the James River in May. Its voyage followed the course of one of the three ships that brought the first English colonists. Special exhibits at Jamestown Settlement highlighted the experiences of the American Indians, Europeans, and Africans who lived in and around the colony.

Queen Elizabeth II (center) of the United Kingdom takes part in the celebration of Jamestown's 400th anniversary in 2007.

In a sense, Jamestown's 400th anniversary (quadricentennial) was America's 400th anniversary. An honored guest at the opening festivities was the United Kingdom's Queen Elizabeth II. She had last visited Virginia 50 years before, in 1957, when Jim Crow laws were still in force. Now she saw the state transformed. People of all races mingled. Virginia's diversity was reflected in each pageant and exhibit.

After a visit to Jamestown, the queen spoke to the Virginia General Assembly. "The melting pot metaphor captures one of the great strengths of your country," she said. "[It] is an inspiration to others around the world as we face the continuing social challenges ahead."

READ ABOUT

A crowd enjoys a sunny day at Virginia Beach.

PEOPLE

★

VIRGINIANS ARE PASSIONATE ABOUT THEIR STATE'S HISTORY. They are fascinated by Virginia families and ancestors; by Virginia generals, heroes, and presidents; and by the details of the state's role in the Civil War. Black Virginians take special pride in the brave efforts of Gabriel Prosser and Nat Turner to defeat slavery. And many Virginians enjoy continuing the refined and gracious example set by 19th-century hosts such as Dolley Madison.

Members of a 4-H group in Bluemont working with llamas

WHO'S A VIRGINIAN?

In 2006, Virginia had 7,642,884 people. It ranked 12th in population among the states. According to a 2005 estimate, most Virginians (68.2 percent) classified themselves as white. Another 6 percent reported Hispanic ancestry. Almost one of every five Virginians is African American. Some 4.6 percent are of Asian descent. Many of these people are immigrants from Vietnam and Cambodia who have settled in northern Virginia. Another 0.3 percent are of Native Hawaiian or Pacific Island heritage. About three of every 1,000 Virginians is Native American. About 1.6 percent of Virginians describe themselves as belonging to two or more races.

Where Virginians Live

The colors on this map indicate population density throughout the state. The darker the color, the more people live there.

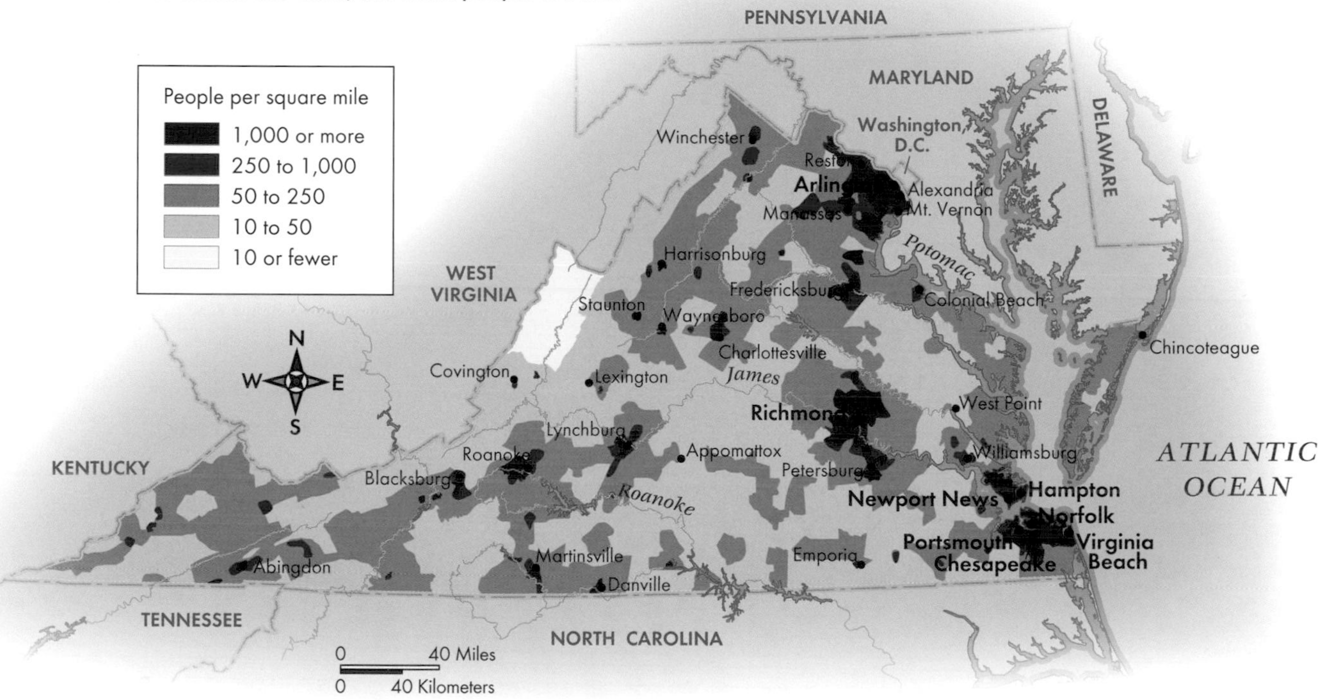

People per square mile
- 1,000 or more
- 250 to 1,000
- 50 to 250
- 10 to 50
- 10 or fewer

People QuickFacts

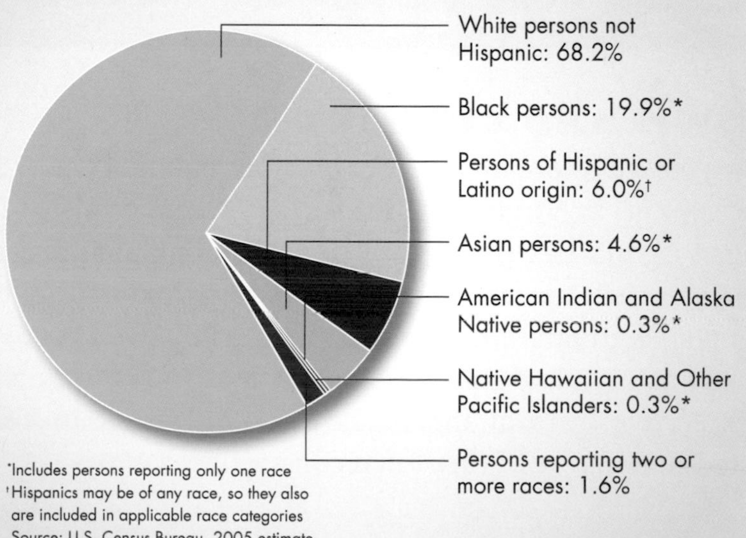

*Includes persons reporting only one race
†Hispanics may be of any race, so they also are included in applicable race categories
Source: U.S. Census Bureau, 2005 estimate

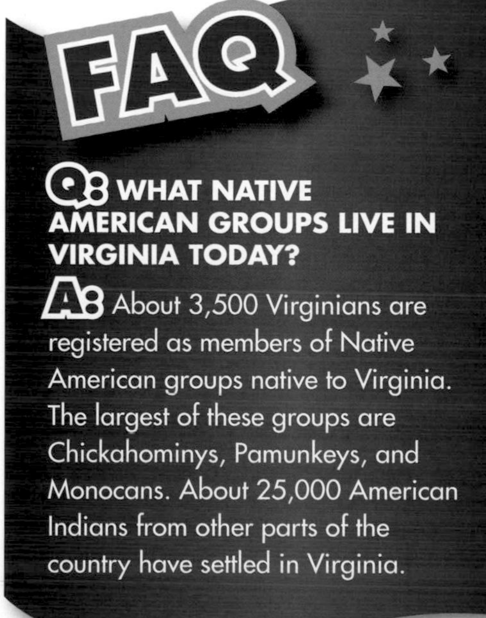

FAQ

Q: WHAT NATIVE AMERICAN GROUPS LIVE IN VIRGINIA TODAY?

A: About 3,500 Virginians are registered as members of Native American groups native to Virginia. The largest of these groups are Chickahominys, Pamunkeys, and Monocans. About 25,000 American Indians from other parts of the country have settled in Virginia.

A mother and daughter browse in a Newport News gift shop.

TOWN AND COUNTRY

On average, there are 193 persons per square mile (75 per sq km) in Virginia. But this figure can be misleading. Virginia has some very densely populated areas and some places where few people live. About 73 percent of Virginians are urban dwellers. They live in cities or towns of at least 2,500 people. The rest of Virginia's people live in rural areas. They live on farms, in forested regions, or in tiny towns and villages.

More than 65 percent of all Virginians are packed into three main metropolitan areas: Richmond and its suburbs; the Virginia suburbs of Washington, D.C.; and Hampton Roads. Thousands of people from Arlington and Alexandria commute every day to jobs in the nation's capital. Although they live in Virginia, they often look to Washington for cultural activities. Yet when they get home, they enjoy a gentler, more southern pace of life.

Big City Life

This list shows the population of Virginia's biggest cities.

Virginia Beach........435,619
Norfolk.............229,112
Chesapeake..........220,560
Richmond............192,913
Newport News.......178,281

Source: U.S. Census Bureau, 2006 estimate

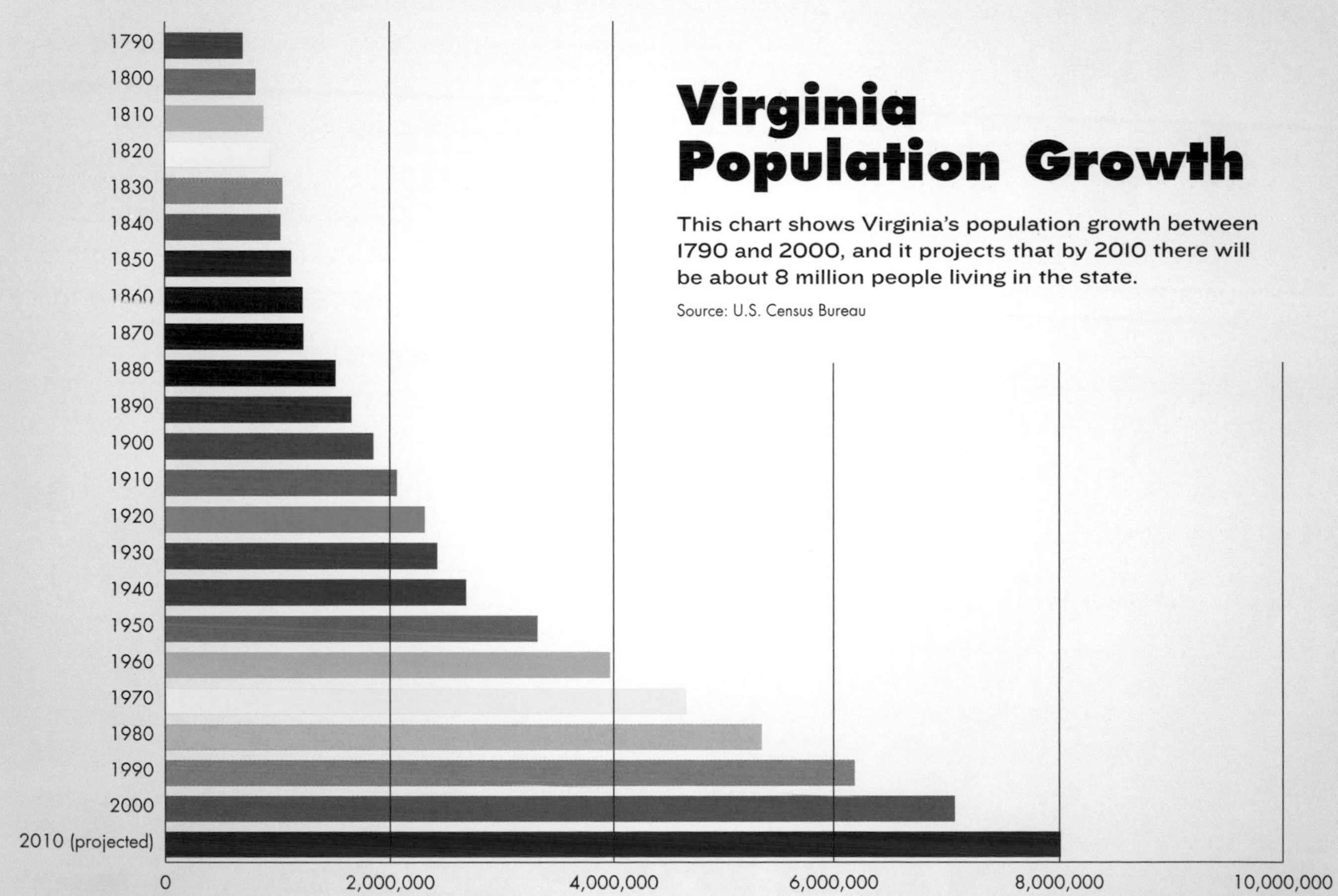

Virginia Population Growth

This chart shows Virginia's population growth between 1790 and 2000, and it projects that by 2010 there will be about 8 million people living in the state.

Source: U.S. Census Bureau

WOW

The first peanuts grown in North America were planted in Virginia. Portuguese traders brought peanuts to the colony in the 1600s.

HOW TO TALK LIKE A VIRGINIAN

Virginians often say that it's easy to pick out a Tidewater accent. People from the Tidewater use some unique words that trace back to the early English settlers.

"Salett" refers to green vegetables such as collard greens or spinach. In western Virginia, a backpack or purse is called a kit. If a man wants to marry a woman, he "woos" her.

HOW TO EAT LIKE A VIRGINIAN

With its miles of coast fronting Chesapeake Bay and the Atlantic Ocean, Virginia is a great place to go for seafood. Chesapeake Bay crab cakes, served with a dash of lemon or tartar sauce, are always a favorite. Oysters can be fried, baked, or eaten raw.

Virginia is especially famous for two foods: ham and peanuts. Delicious smoked hams are shipped all over the world from the town of Smithfield. Tidewater peanuts are the largest and plumpest peanuts grown in the United States.

Serving up crab, oysters, and other great food from the Chesapeake Bay

MENU

WHAT'S ON THE MENU IN VIRGINIA?

Collard greens

Steamed Collard Greens

Collard greens are tangy, tasty, and good for you. They are often cooked with spinach or turnip greens and served as "mixed greens." Black-eyed peas can be added for texture and flavor.

Fried Chicken

Chicken pieces are coated with flour, seasoned with salt, and sizzled to a crisp in hot oil.

Brunswick Stew

This is a hearty mix of meat chunks, vegetables, and gravy. According to legend, Brunswick stew originated in Brunswick County in 1828. In bygone days, it was cooked with squirrel, rabbit, or other game.

Corn Bread and Biscuits

These can be served with gravy, butter, or honey.

TRY THIS RECIPE
Apple Brown Betty

Virginia is a major apple-growing state, and it has developed some wonderful apple dishes. Here's a delicious dessert that you might enjoy. Be sure to ask an adult to help.

Ingredients:

2 cups diced, peeled apples
2 cups bread crumbs
¾ cup brown sugar
2 tablespoons melted butter
¼ teaspoon cinnamon
¼ cup hot water

Instructions:

1. Preheat oven to 350°. Mix together the bread crumbs and melted butter.
2. Place half of the apples in a greased 8 x 8-inch baking pan. Cover with bread crumb mixture and half of the brown sugar. Repeat and sprinkle cinnamon over the top.
3. Add hot water and cover with foil.
4. Bake for 30 minutes.
5. Remove foil (ask an adult to help; the foil will be hot, and there might be a lot of steam). Bake for a few more minutes, until the top is brown.
6. Serve with ice cream or whipped cream.

Corn bread with honey and butter

A quilt display in Leesburg

CRAFTS

In the mountains of western Virginia, people once made nearly everything they used in their homes. Today, craftspeople keep alive the skills that have been passed down through the generations. Carpenters build beautiful cabinets, chests, and tables. Carved wooden bowls and utensils are elegant and graceful. Handmade musical instruments include fiddles, banjos, **dulcimers**, and drums and are decorated with carvings.

Potters in Virginia use local clays to make dishes, pitchers, and other useful objects for the home. Some potters create works that are purely decorative, such as sculpted wall hangings. Quilters draw on traditional patterns and develop designs of their own as well.

Every year, Virginia sponsors a series of arts and crafts festivals around the state. From Virginia Beach to

WORD TO KNOW

dulcimers *musical instruments with three or four strings, traditionally played in the Appalachian region of the United States*

Floyd in the far southwest, there are opportunities to see the work of talented craftspeople. And if you miss the festivals, there's another way to find Virginia crafts. Today, craftspeople are marketing their centuries-old traditions over the Internet!

SCULPTURE AND PAINTING

Virginia has been home to a number of outstanding sculptors and painters. Edward V. Valentine was born in Richmond in 1838. He studied art in Europe and returned to Richmond to open a studio. In the years after the Civil War, he carved marble busts of many of the Confederate generals, including Stonewall Jackson and Pierre Beauregard. His large marble figure of Robert E. Lee can be seen at the chapel of Washington and Lee University.

Moses Ezekiel was also a Richmond native. He attended the Virginia Military Institute and later served in the Civil War. He was wounded at the Battle of New Market and defended Richmond from the final Union assault. In 1869, he moved to Europe, where he became a successful sculptor. Though he spent the rest of his life in Germany and Italy, Ezekiel never forgot his Virginia roots. His memorial statue, *Virginia Mourning Her Dead*, honoring 10 cadets killed at the Battle of New Market, stands at the Virginia Military Institute.

Virginia painter George Caleb Bingham was born in Augusta

ROBERT MILLS: CELEBRATIONS IN STONE

As an aspiring young architect, Robert Mills (1781–1855) was a great admirer of Thomas Jefferson. Mills designed houses in Richmond, Baltimore, and Philadelphia. His most enduring creation is the Washington Monument in the nation's capital. He is considered by some to have been the America's first native-born architect.

Want to know more? See www.philadelphiabuildings.org/pab/app/ar_display.cfm/27071

Virginia has more than 1 million students in its public schools, from kindergarten through 12th grade.

County and went west with his family as a boy. He painted vivid scenes of frontier life on the Missouri River. Draftsman and painter Jerome Myers grew up in Petersburg. As a young man, he moved to New York City, where he captured scenes of early 20th-century immigrant life on canvas and on paper.

GOING TO SCHOOL

In 1870, Virginia passed a law to create free public schools throughout the state. Today, all children must go to school from ages 5 to 17. In 2005, 1.19 million students were enrolled in Virginia's public schools between kindergarten and 12th grade.

Virginia is known around the world for its outstanding colleges and universities. The College of William and Mary, founded in Williamsburg in 1693, is the second-oldest college in the United States. Only Harvard University in Massachusetts is older.

WORLDS OF WORDS

Have you ever heard the spooky poem that begins, "Once upon a midnight dreary, While I pondered, weak and weary"? "The Raven" is one of the most famous poems in the English language. And it was written by a Virginian, Edgar Allan Poe! Poe grew up in 19th-century Richmond. Although he lived in many other places, he always claimed Virginia as his true home. Many of his stories deal with the supernatural and with the dark side of human nature. Stories such as "The Gold-Bug" and "The Murders in the Rue Morgue" were some of the first detective stories published in the United States.

Like Poe, Ellen Glasgow was raised in Richmond. She published her first novel, *The Descendant*, in 1897. Most of her books deal with Virginia families and the struggles of a changing society. Glasgow was sometimes criticized as being too smart and strong for a proper Virginia lady. She didn't let such comments stop her! Her novel *In This Our Life* won the Pulitzer Prize in 1942.

Novelist and essayist William Styron grew up in Newport News, less than 100 miles (161 km) from the site of Nat Turner's slave rebellion. Styron's 1967 novel, *The Confessions of Nat Turner*, tells the story of the 1831 uprising from Turner's point of view. In addition to writing award-winning novels, he published a memoir in 1990, *Darkness Visible*, about his battle with severe depression.

MINI-BIO

KATHERINE PATERSON: THE WOMAN WHO CREATED TERABITHIA

Katherine Paterson's (1932–) missionary family moved from China to Winchester at the outbreak of World War II. After she grew up, Paterson taught school for a year in rural Lovettsville, then spent four years in Japan. After returning to the United States, she decided to try writing novels for young readers. Her award-winning books include *Jacob Have I Loved*, about a Chesapeake Bay family, and *Bridge to Terabithia*, about two friends in rural southwest Virginia.

Want to know more? See www.childrensbookguild.org/paterson.html

REMEMBERING MISTY

If you love books about horses, you may have read *Misty of Chincoteague* by Marguerite Henry (1902–1997). The book tells the story of two children from Chincoteague Island who tame a wild pony from Assateague. Henry based the novel on her family's adventures taming a wild Assateague colt. She wrote many other novels about horses for young readers. Misty's story continued in *Sea Star, Orphan of Chincoteague* and *Stormy, Misty's Foal*.

The Carter Family included Maybelle (seated) and her daughters (left to right), June, Anita, and Helen.

MAKING MUSIC

In 1927, three musicians from Maces Springs in Scott County made their first recording. They were A. P. Carter, his wife, Sara, and his sister-in-law Maybelle Carter. The Carter Family sang old-time country songs, accompanied by guitar and autoharp. Their music became wildly popular in the 1930s and won a nationwide audience for the traditional music of the Appalachian region. Maybelle later went on to perform with her three daughters, Helen, June, and Anita. The Carters are considered to be the "First Family of Country Music."

Another performer who helped make country music popular was Patsy Cline of Winchester. During the late 1950s, she had several hit songs, including "Walkin' After Midnight" and "I Fall to Pieces." She died in a plane crash when she was only 31 years old. She lives on as a legend of the country music scene.

Growing up on the streets of Portsmouth, Missy Elliott used to stand on trash cans and sing to passersby. She got her first recording contract as a teenager, and she

WOW

The Wolf Trap National Park for the Performing Arts is the only national park in the United States devoted to the performing arts.

quickly soared to the top of the hip-hop charts. Albums such as *Da Real World* crackle with her street-smart fierceness.

Whatever sort of music you like, you can hear it at the Wolf Trap Foundation for the Performing Arts in Vienna. It hosts musical events throughout the year. They include the Louisiana Swamp Romp (Cajun), Washington Irish Folk Festival (Celtic), and Ricky Skaggs' Pickin' Party (bluegrass)—and that's only a sampling! If you like classical music, you can go to operas, ballets, and symphonies at Wolf Trap's magnificent Filene Center.

Damian Marley performing at Wolf Trap's Filene Center

MINI-BIO

ELLA FITZGERALD: THE FIRST LADY OF SONG

Born in Newport News, Ella Fitzgerald (1918–1990) grew up in Yonkers, New York. As a teenager, she got into trouble with the law and even spent some time in a reformatory. Then, when she was 17, her life changed forever. She won a singing contest at New York's Apollo Theater, and her career took off! Over the next 57 years, she was recognized as one of the finest jazz singers in the world. In her personal life, she was very shy. Onstage her shyness disappeared, and she sang with great power.

Want to know more? See www.pbs.org/wnet/americanmasters/database/fitzgerald_e.html

The Virginia Tech Hokies celebrate a win over the Virginia Cavaliers in Charlottesville in 2007.

GETTING OUT TO PLAY

Virginia has no professional teams, but that doesn't stop Virginians from being passionate about sports. During football season, most Virginians root for the Washington Redskins, headquartered in Loudoun County. Virginia's baseball fans follow "the Nats," the Washington Nationals. The Richmond Braves are Virginia's popular minor-league team.

College teams make headlines all over Virginia. The Cavaliers of the University of Virginia (women's lacrosse) fill the stands with cheering spectators. Men's soccer and football are big at Virginia Tech, where crowds cheer for the Hokies.

SEE IT HERE!

VIRGINIA SPORTS HALL OF FAME

In 2005, the Virginia Sports Hall of Fame and Museum opened in downtown Portsmouth. Displays honor the state's high school and college athletes. In the Auto Racing Hall, you can experience the speed of the NASCAR track in a computer racing simulator. There are plenty of other hands-on opportunities, too, in the sports complex. It offers interactive exhibits related to baseball, football, and soccer.

The great outdoors is Virginia's finest sports arena. The lakes and rivers are made for fishing, swimming, and waterskiing. Virginians enjoy sailing and deep-sea fishing along the coast. The state's parks and recreation areas offer thousands of miles of hiking trails. Hikers are drawn to Virginia's portion of the Appalachian Trail, which snakes down the nation's east coast from Maine to Georgia. The trail enters Virginia east of Winchester and leaves the state near Mount Rogers.

Biking in Shenandoah National Park

MINI-BIO

ARTHUR ASHE: TENNIS WAS HIS GAME

When he was 10, Richmond's Arthur Ashe (1943–1993) caught the attention of a tennis coach, who arranged for him to have lessons. In 1963, Ashe became the first African American player ever named to the U.S. Davis Cup team. In 1968, he helped create the United States Tennis Association to encourage young, inner-city athletes. He retired from professional tennis in 1980, having won three Grand Slam events. Ashe spoke out against racial injustice and helped the American Heart Association and organizations that worked to combat HIV/AIDS. He died of complications from AIDS. In his honor, the U.S. Open finals are played at New York's Arthur Ashe Stadium.

Want to know more? See www.vahistorical.org/sva2003/ashe.htm

READ ABOUT

Voters line up outside a community house in Arlington to vote in a presidential election.

GOVERNMENT

★

IN 2007, VIRGINIA'S GENERAL ASSEMBLY REJECTED A BILL TO MAKE APPLES THE STATE FRUIT. Fourth graders from a Fairfax elementary school had proposed it. A reporter quipped, "A proposal to make the apple the Virginia State Fruit turned rotten yesterday." But Kristen Amundson, a member of the General Assembly, wasn't laughing. She explained, "I care passionately . . . that even fourth graders understand that elected officials have to take you seriously and pay attention to you because you are a citizen of the commonwealth."

FAQ

Q: HOW MANY STATES ARE CALLED COMMONWEALTHS?

A: Virginia is one of only four states that is officially called a commonwealth. The others are Massachusetts, Pennsylvania, and Kentucky.

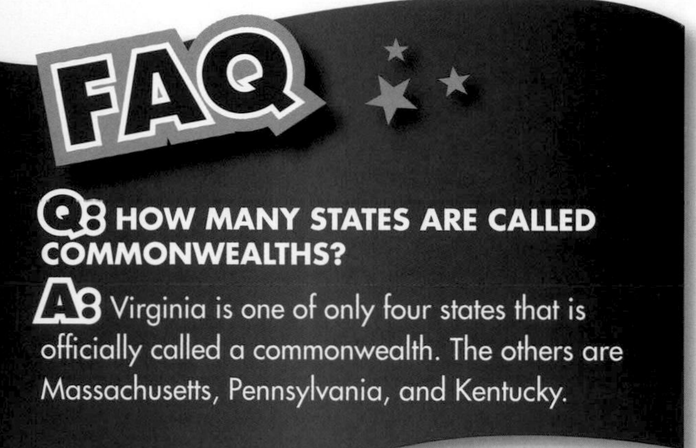

WORD TO KNOW

commonwealth *a government that works for the common good, or the common consent, of the people*

THE STRUCTURE OF GOVERNMENT

Virginia's present constitution went into effect in 1971. It divides the state government into three branches. The legislative branch, or General Assembly, passes the laws. The judicial branch, or court system, interprets the laws. The executive branch, or office of the governor, makes sure that the laws are carried out.

Capital City

This map shows places of interest in Richmond, Virginia's capital city.

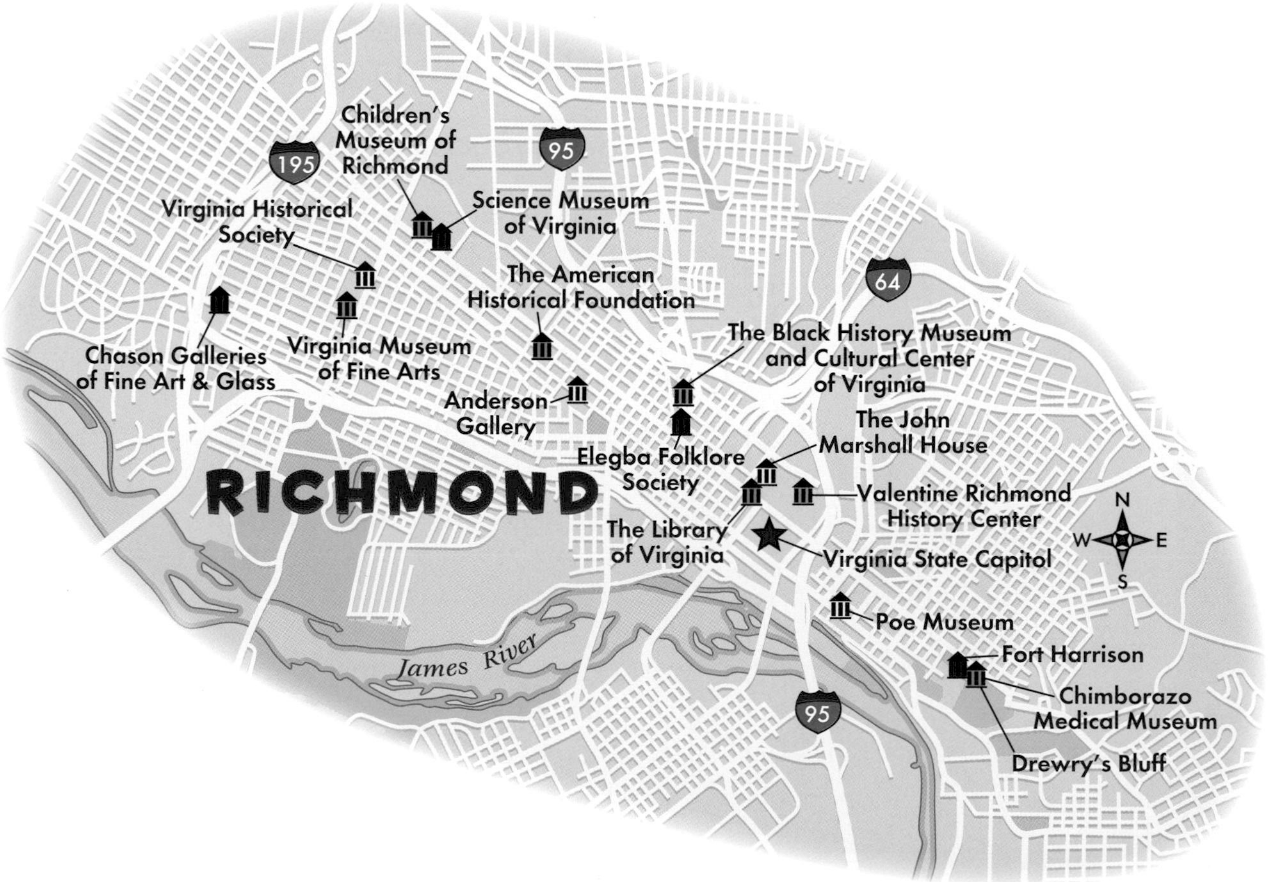

195
95
64
95
Children's Museum of Richmond
Science Museum of Virginia
Virginia Historical Society
The American Historical Foundation
Chason Galleries of Fine Art & Glass
Virginia Museum of Fine Arts
Anderson Gallery
The Black History Museum and Cultural Center of Virginia
The John Marshall House
Elegba Folklore Society
Valentine Richmond History Center
The Library of Virginia
Virginia State Capitol
Poe Museum
Fort Harrison
Chimborazo Medical Museum
Drewry's Bluff
RICHMOND
James River
N
W
E
S

The state capitol in Richmond

THE LEGISLATIVE BRANCH

Virginia's General Assembly is divided into two houses. The upper house, with 40 members, is called the senate. The 100-member lower house is known as the house of delegates. The General Assembly meets in the state capitol in Richmond.

THE JUDICIAL BRANCH

The court system in Virginia has several tiers. The lowest courts in the state are juvenile and domestic relations courts and general district courts. The General Assembly elects judges to serve six-year terms on these lower courts.

Capitol Facts

Here are some fascinating facts about Virginia's state capitol.

- Virginia's capitol in Richmond was designed by Thomas Jefferson. He modeled the building on a Roman temple in southern France.
- Virginia's General Assembly first met in the present capitol in 1788.
- Colonial Virginia had eight other capitols before the present one was built.
- Virginia's capitol is one of 13 statehouses in the United States that does not have an exterior dome.
- In 1870, a gallery in a second-floor courtroom collapsed, causing the collapse of the floor below. Sixty-two people were killed, including a grandson of Patrick Henry.
- The largest room in the capitol is the Old House of Delegates. It is 86 feet (26 m) wide and now serves as a museum.

MINI-BIO

JOHN MARSHALL: LAYING DOWN THE LAW

John Marshall (1755–1835) grew up in a log cabin in Fauquier County. After fighting in the American Revolution, he became a lawyer. President John Adams recognized his diplomacy and clear thinking, and appointed him secretary of state. In 1801, Marshall became chief justice, or head, of the Supreme Court. He made key decisions about how to interpret the new U.S. Constitution, including that courts have the right to reject laws that go against the Constitution. He served until his death, and his opinions are still respected today.

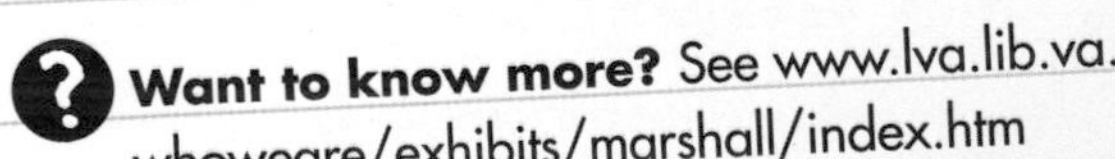

Want to know more? See www.lva.lib.va.us/whoweare/exhibits/marshall/index.htm

WEIRD LAWS IN VIRGINIA

Virginia has some pretty wacky laws. Can you believe these are still on the books?

- In Richmond, it is illegal to flip a coin in a restaurant to decide who buys a cup of coffee.
- Citizens must honk their horn when passing other cars.
- Children may not go trick-or-treating on Halloween.
- No animal except the raccoon may be hunted on Sundays.

Cases from the lower courts can be appealed to the circuit court. From there, a case can be appealed to the court of appeals. Circuit court and court of appeals judges are elected to eight-year terms by the General Assembly.

The supreme court is the highest court in Virginia. The General Assembly elects seven judges, or justices, to serve on the supreme court. The justices serve 12-year terms. The chief justice is the justice who has been on the court the longest.

THE EXECUTIVE BRANCH

The people of Virginia elect their governor to a four-year term. The governor is not allowed to hold office for two terms in a row. A lieutenant governor is also elected. He or she takes over if the governor resigns or dies in office. Another high-level elected official is the attorney general.

Representing Virginia

This list shows the number of elected officials who represent Virginia, both on the state and national levels.

OFFICE	NUMBER	LENGTH OF TERM
State senators	40	4 years
State delegates	100	2 years
U.S. senators	2	6 years
U.S. representatives	11	2 years
Presidential electors	13	—

Virginia State Government

EXECUTIVE BRANCH

Carries out state laws

Lieutenant Governor

Governor

Attorney General

Governor's Cabinet

Secretary of Commonwealth
Secretary of Administration
Secretary of Agriculture and Forestry
Secretary of Education
Secretary of Finance
Secretary of Health and Human Services
Secretary of Natural Resources
Secretary of Technology
Secretary of Transportation
Chief of Staff

Secretary of Commerce and Trade
Assistant to the Governor for Commonwealth Preparedness
Senior Advisor to the Governor for Workforce

Department heads of:
Accounts
Aviation
Transportation
Finance
and many more

LEGISLATIVE BRANCH

Makes and passes state laws

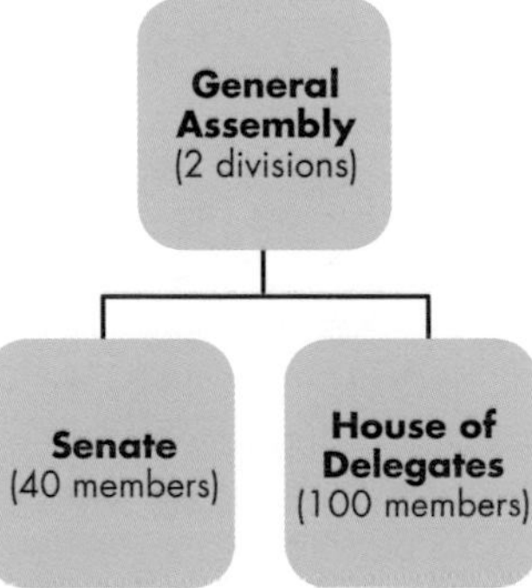

JUDICIAL BRANCH

Enforces state laws

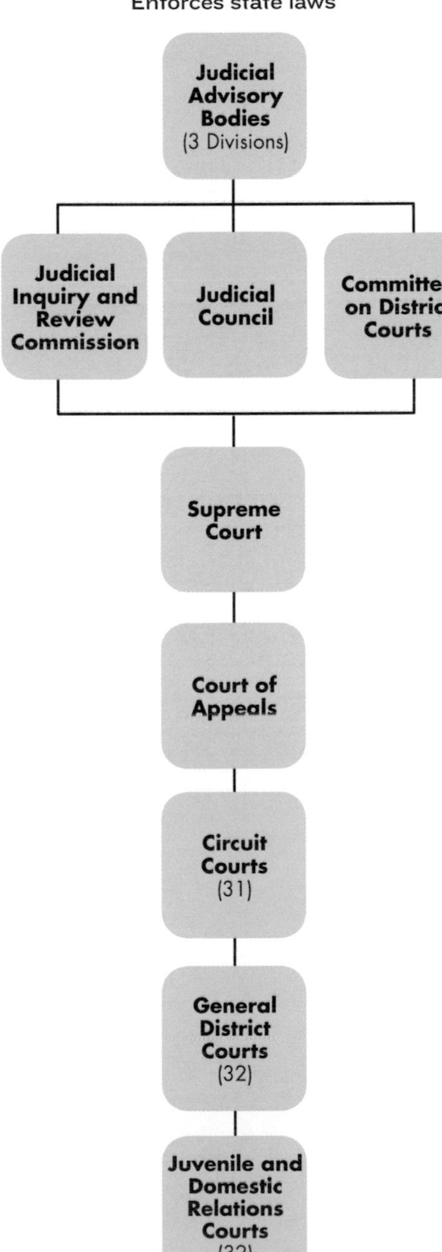

Virginia's Executive Mansion is the oldest occupied governor's mansion in the nation. Virginia governors have been living there since 1813!

The governor of Virginia appoints most of the top officials in the state. In this way, he or she has tremendous influence on the state's policies. More than 40 executive departments serve Virginia's citizens, including education, environmental quality, state police, taxation, and transportation.

LOCAL GOVERNMENT

Virginia is divided into 95 counties. Nearly all Virginia counties are governed by a board of supervisors. The voters generally choose county officials such as a commissioner of revenue, a treasurer, a sheriff, and a county clerk.

Virginia Counties

This map shows the 95 counties in Virginia. Richmond, the state capital, is indicated with a star.

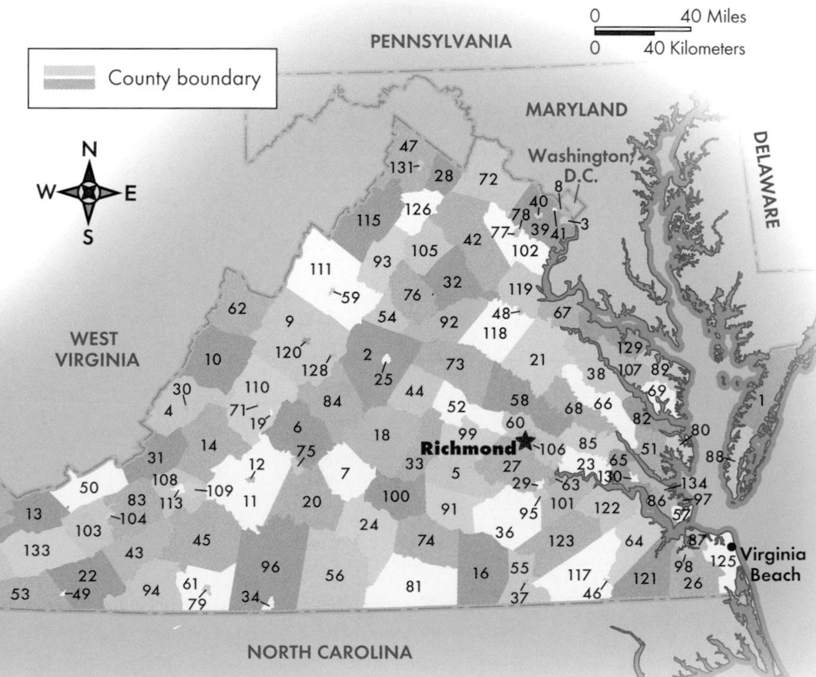

1. ACCOMACK
2. ALBEMARLE
3. ALEXANDRIA CITY
4. ALLEGHANY
5. AMELIA
6. AMHERST
7. APPOMATTOX
8. ARLINGTON
9. AUGUSTA
10. BATH
11. BEDFORD
12. BEDFORD CITY
13. BLAND
14. BOTETOURT
15. BRISTOL CITY
16. BRUNSWICK
17. BUCHANAN
18. BUCKINGHAM
19. BUENA VISTA CITY
20. CAMPBELL
21. CAROLINE
22. CARROLL
23. CHARLES CITY
24. CHARLOTTE
25. CHARLOTTESVILLE CITY
26. CHESAPEAKE CITY
27. CHESTERFIELD
28. CLARKE
29. COLONIAL HEIGHTS CITY
30. COVINGTON CITY
31. CRAIG
32. CULPEPER
33. CUMBERLAND
34. DANVILLE CITY
35. DICKENSON
36. DINWIDDIE
37. EMPORIA CITY
38. ESSEX
39. FAIRFAX
40. FAIRFAX CITY
41. FALLS CHURCH CITY
42. FAUQUIER
43. FLOYD
44. FLUVANNA
45. FRANKLIN
46. FRANKLIN CITY
47. FREDERICK
48. FREDERICKSBURG CITY
49. GALAX CITY
50. GILES
51. GLOUCESTER
52. GOOCHLAND
53. GRAYSON
54. GREENE
55. GREENSVILLE
56. HALIFAX
57. HAMPTON CITY
58. HANOVER
59. HARRISONBURG CITY
60. HENRICO
61. HENRY
62. HIGHLAND
63. HOPEWELL CITY
64. ISLE OF WIGHT
65. JAMES CITY
66. KING AND QUEEN
67. KING GEORGE
68. KING WILLIAM
69. LANCASTER
70. LEE
71. LEXINGTON CITY
72. LOUDOUN
73. LOUISA
74. LUNENBURG
75. LYNCHBURG CITY
76. MADISON
77. MANASSAS CITY
78. MANASSAS PARK CITY
79. MARTINSVILLE CITY
80. MATHEWS
81. MECKLENBURG
82. MIDDLESEX
83. MONTGOMERY
84. NELSON
85. NEW KENT
86. NEWPORT NEWS CITY
87. NORFOLK CITY
88. NORTHAMPTON
89. NORTHUMBERLAND
90. NORTON CITY
91. NOTTOWAY
92. ORANGE
93. PAGE
94. PATRICK
95. PETERSBURG CITY
96. PITTSYLVANIA
97. POQUOSON CITY
98. PORTSMOUTH CITY
99. POWHATAN
100. PRINCE EDWARD
101. PRINCE GEORGE
102. PRINCE WILLIAM
103. PULASKI
104. RADFORD CITY
105. RAPPAHANNOCK
106. RICHMOND CITY
107. RICHMOND
108. ROANOKE
109. ROANOKE CITY
110. ROCKBRIDGE
111. ROCKINGHAM
112. RUSSELL
113. SALEM CITY
114. SCOTT
115. SHENANDOAH
116. SMYTH
117. SOUTHAMPTON
118. SPOTSYLVANIA
119. STAFFORD
120. STAUNTON CITY
121. SUFFOLK CITY
122. SURRY
123. SUSSEX
124. TAZEWELL
125. VIRGINIA BEACH CITY
126. WARREN
127. WASHINGTON
128. WAYNESBORO CITY
129. WESTMORELAND
130. WILLIAMSBURG CITY
131. WINCHESTER CITY
132. WISE
133. WYTHE
134. YORK

MINI-BIO

L. DOUGLAS WILDER: A MISSION FOR CHANGE

The grandson of former slaves, L. Douglas Wilder (1931–) wanted to make the world a better place for all people. A law career led him to Virginia politics. In 1970, he was elected to the Virginia senate, where he served for 16 years. He worked for fair housing laws and better job opportunities for minorities. He was elected lieutenant governor in 1985 and governor in 1989. Wilder was America's first African American governor.

Want to know more? See www.vahistorical.org/sva2003/wilder.htm

Any town in Virginia that has 5,000 people or more can vote to become an independent city. About 40 towns have decided to take this step. An independent city sets up its own government. This city government is completely separate from that of the county where the city is found.

Virginia has produced eight U.S. presidents, more than any other state!

VIRGINIA PRESIDENTS

George Washington (1732–1799) was the nation's first president (1789–1797). See Mini-Bio, page 44.

Thomas Jefferson (1743–1826) was the third president of the United States (1801–1809). See Mini-Bio, page 45.

James Madison (1751–1836), called the Father of the Constitution, served as fourth president of the United States (1809–1817). He was president during the War of 1812 with Great Britain, when British troops invaded Washington and burned down the White House.

James Monroe (1755–1831) was the fifth president of the United States (1817–1825). He is best known for his Monroe Doctrine, which stated that the United States would defend the nations of the Western Hemisphere from invasion by foreign powers.

William Henry Harrison (1773–1841) earned fame by fighting in the Indian wars on the frontier. He became the ninth U.S. president (1841). He died of pneumonia after only one month in office.

John Tyler (1790–1862) served as governor of Virginia and held a seat in the U.S. Senate. When William Henry Harrison died, Tyler became the 10th president of the United States (1841–1845).

Zachary Taylor (1784–1850) earned the nickname "Old Rough 'n' Ready" during the Mexican-American War. He became the 12th president of the United States (1849–1850), but died in office after only a year.

Woodrow Wilson (1856–1924), born in Staunton, was the 28th U.S. president (1913–1921). He tried to keep the United States out of World War I, but found that impossible.

State Flag

In 1861, the Virginia State Convention passed an ordinance establishing a design almost exactly the same as the one in use today. This flag has a deep blue field with a circular white center that features the state seal.

State Seal

The state seal was adopted in 1776. It features the state motto, *Sic semper tyrannis* (Latin for "Thus Always to Tyrants"). Two people are shown acting out the meaning of the motto. Both are dressed as warriors. The woman, Virtue, represents Virginia. The man on the ground is holding a chain, which shows that he is a tyrant. His fallen crown lies nearby.

READ ABOUT

Employees share information in the operations center at the Central Intelligence Agency.

ECONOMY

★

A FISHER CASTS HIS NETS ON CHESAPEAKE BAY. A horse rancher stands beside a fence, admiring a lively herd of spring colts. Teachers grade tests and prepare lesson plans in their rural school. An army officer ponders the world situation while stuck in a traffic jam on the way to work at the Pentagon. All of these people are Virginians. All of them help make Virginia the economically diverse state that it is today.

Doctors and other medical professionals are some of the many service workers in Virginia.

SERVICE INDUSTRIES

The next time you log on to the Internet, think about the service provider you use. If you use AOL (formerly America OnLine), you are connecting to a Virginia company. AOL, one of the nation's biggest Internet providers, is based in the Virginia city of Dulles. High-tech industries play an important part in Virginia's economy.

Service industries account for the largest portion of Virginia's **gross state product**. People who work in the service industries do things for others. Waiters, salesclerks, bankers, teachers, doctors, and police officers all are service industry workers.

WORD TO KNOW

gross state product *the total value of all the goods and services produced in a state*

Economists group the service industries into several broad categories. In Virginia, the biggest category is called community, business, and personal services. It includes everything from telephone repair crews to highway engineers and computer consultants. Virginia's high-tech businesses keep this part of the economy booming.

The second-largest part of the service economy is the grouping called finance, insurance, and real estate. In the 1990s and early 2000s, the housing market surged in northern Virginia. More and more people wanted to live there because they worked in government offices in or near Washington, D.C. Virginia has major banking centers in Falls Church and Richmond.

MINI-BIO

MAGGIE LENA WALKER: BANK PRESIDENT

Maggie Lena Walker (1867–1934) grew up in Richmond. For several years, she taught school, then did volunteer work while she was raising a family. In 1903, she formed St. Luke's Penny Savings Bank in Richmond. She served as its president until 1932. She was the first woman bank president in the United States. In 1931, her bank merged with several other African American–owned banks to form the Consolidated Bank and Trust Company. Walker lectured and wrote extensively about finance and race relations.

Want to know more? See www.nps.gov/malw/home.htm

This real estate agent meets with prospective buyers in Richmond.

SEE IT HERE!

THE CIA

Agents from the Central Intelligence Agency (CIA) are at work all over the world. The CIA is one of the world's largest **intelligence** organizations. Its headquarters stands on 250 acres (100 ha) of land in McLean. The main building has an exhibit center with a collection of historic equipment that has been used in espionage operations. On display are tiny surveillance cameras and microphones that can be ingeniously concealed. But if you want to see the exhibits, you'll have to become a CIA employee. The exhibit center is not open to the public.

Government services are the third-biggest part of the service industries in Virginia. This category includes workers in federal, state, and local government. Teachers in the public schools, nurses in public hospitals, and generals at the Pentagon are all government employees. Virginia has several important military bases, including Marine Corps Base Quantico and Naval Station Norfolk. These bases employ thousands of people.

Other areas of the service industries in Virginia are trade, transportation, communication, and tourism. Visitors to Virginia help create jobs for restaurant owners, hotel managers, tour guides, and people in many other occupations.

WORD TO KNOW

intelligence *information gathering, spying*

THE BUSINESS OF MAKING THINGS

After the service industries, manufacturing is the next most important portion of Virginia's economy. Factories in Richmond make cigarettes, often from locally grown tobacco. Many Virginia plants make and bottle beer and soft drinks.

Q8 HOW MANY PEOPLE WORK AT CIA HEADQUARTERS?

A8 Estimates put the number at around 17,000. Outside the agency, nobody knows for sure. Even the number of employees is classified information!

Top Products

Agriculture	Broilers, cattle and calves, dairy products, turkeys, nursery and greenhouse products
Manufacturing	Ships, pharmaceutical products, synthetic fabrics, plastics, rubber products, cigarettes, beer, candy
Mining	Coal, sand and gravel
Service	Computer technology, real estate and finance, government and military, wholesale and retail sales

What Do Virginians Do?

This color-coded chart shows what industries Virginians work in.

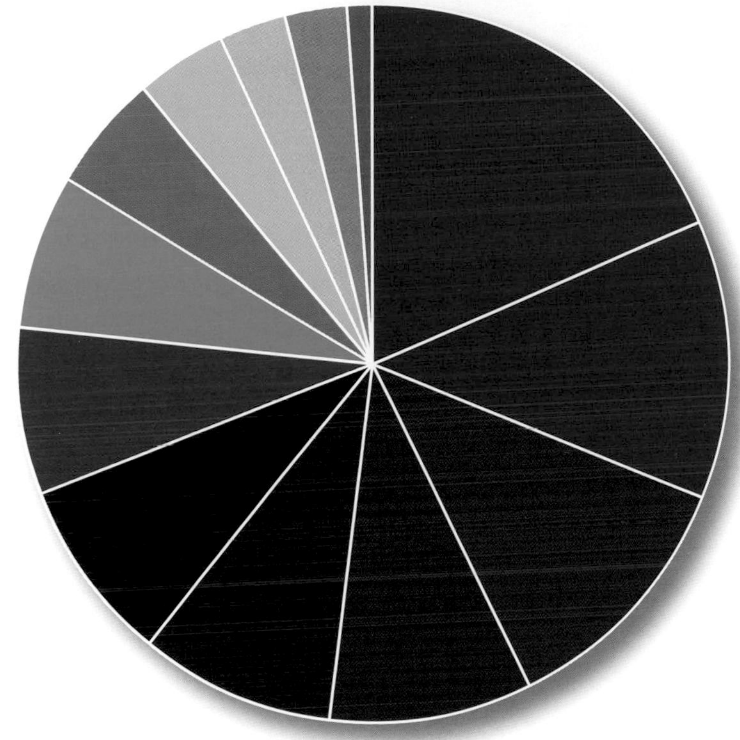

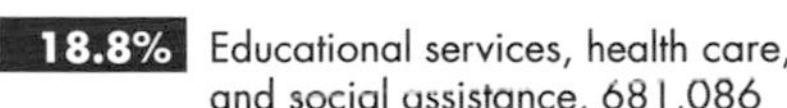

18.8% Educational services, health care, and social assistance, 681,086

12.5% Professional, scientific, and management; administrative and waste management services, 454,802

11.7% Retail trade, 423,386

9.1% Manufacturing, 331,028

8.9% Public administration, 321,417

8.3% Construction, 301,057

7.5% Arts, entertainment, recreation, accommodation, and food services, 273,419

6.9% Finance, insurance, real estate, and rental and leasing, 250,140

5.3% Other services, except public administration, 192,152

4.3% Transportation, warehousing, and utilities, 154,954

3.0% Information, 109,382

2.6% Wholesale trade, 95,591

1.1% Agriculture, forestry, fishing, hunting, and mining, 40,465

Source: U.S. Census Bureau, 2005 estimate

Virginia's chemical industry produces a variety of goods, including medicines and **synthetic** fabrics.

The shipbuilding industry has flourished in Virginia since early in the 20th century. Norfolk, Portsmouth, and Newport News remain major centers for shipbuilding and ship repair. The Norfolk Naval Shipyard in Portsmouth is the largest and oldest shipyard in the

WORD TO KNOW

synthetic *related to something that doesn't occur in nature*

FROM LAND AND SEA

About one-third of Virginia's land is used for farming, but agriculture accounts for less than 1 percent of Virginia's gross state product. Virginia has farms in all parts of the state.

United States. It has workers trained in three dozen trades related to shipbuilding and repair.

If you've got a sweet tooth, Virginia is the place for you! Candy and baked goods are among the many processed foods that come from Virginia. Other manufactured products include plastic and rubber goods. Hundreds of thousands of tires roll out of factories in Danville each year.

Major Agricultural and Mining Products

This map shows where Virginia's major agricultural and mining products come from. See an apple and a pear? That means fruit is found there.

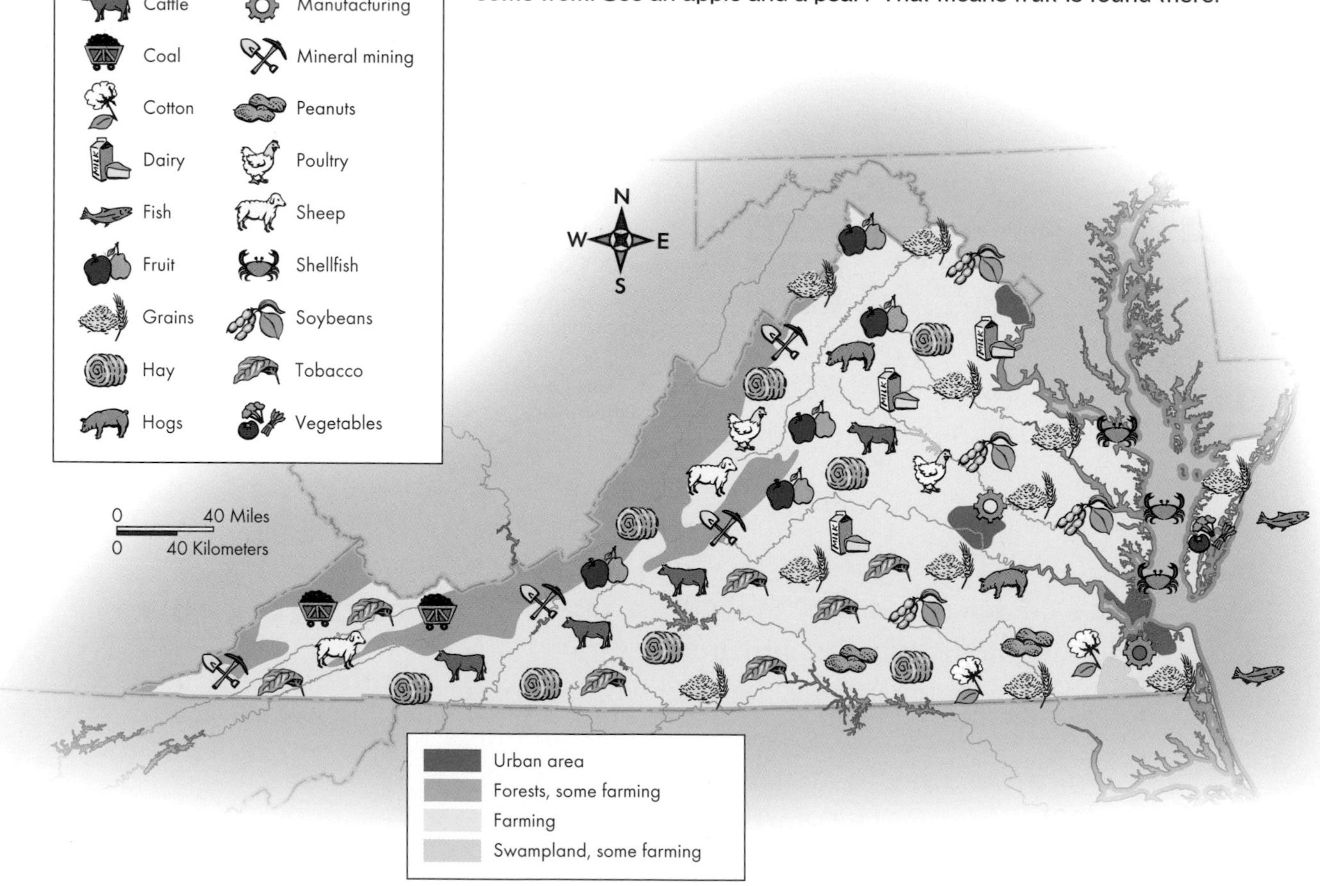

MINI-BIO

CYRUS HALL MCCORMICK: REAPING THE HARVEST

Growing up on a farm in Rockbridge County, Cyrus Hall McCormick (1809–1884) helped each year with the harvest. All of the work had to be done by hand. He was sure he could find an easier way to get the work done. In 1831, he designed and built a mechanical reaping machine. His invention revolutionized farming. With the help of the reaper and later farm machinery, fewer laborers could raise more food.

Want to know more? See at www.vaes.vt.edu/steeles/mccormick/bio.html

For many Virginia farmers, the work year leads to Thanksgiving. That's because they raise a lot of turkeys. The Shenandoah Valley is Virginia's poultry-raising capital. Farmers in the valley also raise tender young chickens called broilers. Cattle are raised in western Virginia. And remember those famous Smithfield hams? The state produces plenty of hogs!

In the colonial days, Virginia's economy rested on tobacco. Today, tobacco is still one of the state's leading crops. Other field crops include corn and soybeans, which are mainly grown along Chesapeake Bay. Virginia farmers also raise tomatoes, potatoes, and sweet potatoes.

Beneath the mountains of southwestern Virginia lie fields of a very different kind—coal. Buchanan and Wise counties are honeycombed with underground coal mines. In the past, thousands of coal miners died of black lung disease, an illness caused by breathing coal dust. Today, miners wear face masks and take many other safety precautions. But coal mining is still hard, dirty, and dangerous work.

Chesapeake Bay and the Atlantic Ocean are home to a rich variety of seafood. Virginia is one of the nation's top producers of crabs and scallops. One of the most important fish caught in Virginia's waters is the small, bony menhaden. Menhaden are a major ingredient in fish meal (used as chicken feed), fish oil, and many fertilizers.

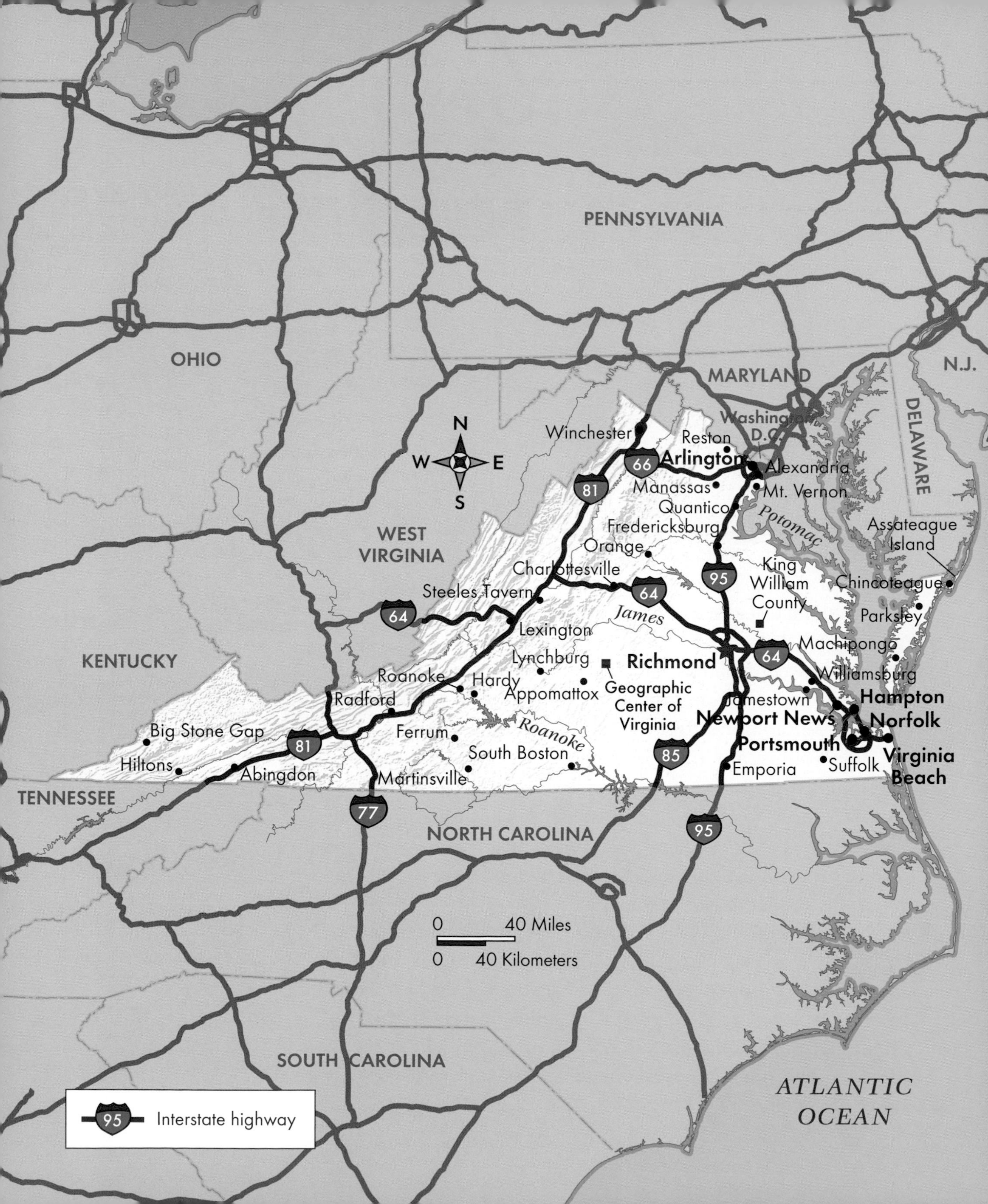

PENNSYLVANIA
OHIO
MARYLAND
N.J.
DELAWARE
Washington D.C.
N
W
E
S
Winchester
Reston
Arlington
Alexandria
Manassas
Mt. Vernon
Quantico
Potomac
Fredericksburg
Assateague Island
WEST VIRGINIA
Orange
Charlottesville
King William County
Chincoteague
Steeles Tavern
Parksley
James
Lexington
Machipongo
KENTUCKY
Lynchburg
Richmond
Williamsburg
Roanoke
Hardy
Appomattox
Geographic Center of Virginia
Hampton
Radford
Jamestown
Newport News
Norfolk
Big Stone Gap
Ferrum
Roanoke
Portsmouth
Virginia Beach
Hiltons
South Boston
Suffolk
Abingdon
Emporia
Martinsville
TENNESSEE
NORTH CAROLINA
66
81
64
95
85
77
0 40 Miles
0 40 Kilometers
SOUTH CAROLINA
ATLANTIC OCEAN
Interstate highway

TRAVEL GUIDE

★

FROM THE CHESAPEAKE BAY SHORES TO THE BLUE RIDGE MOUNTAIN PEAKS, VIRGINIA OFFERS SCENIC BEAUTY, GLIMPSES OF HISTORY, AND PLENTY OF FUN! Visit the homes of presidents, Civil War battlefields, and the oldest English settlements in North America. As you travel through Virginia, you will see natural beauty and human achievement everywhere you go.

← Follow along with this travel map. We'll begin in Arlington and travel all the way west to Appalachia.

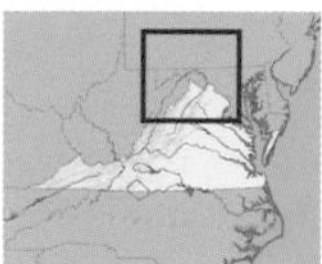

NORTHERN VIRGINIA

THINGS TO DO: Visit Civil War battlefields, follow in the footsteps of George Washington, and look for patriots' names at the "Resting Place of Heroes."

Arlington

★ **Arlington National Cemetery:** Known as the Resting Place of Heroes, this is where more than 200,000 U.S. military men and women are buried.

Visitors to Arlington National Cemetery

Alexandria

★ **Alexandria Black History Museum:** The museum has exhibits on the work, crafts, and lives of African Americans, both before and after the Civil War.

★ **Gadsby's Tavern Museum:** George Washington, Thomas Jefferson, John Adams, and many other Founding Fathers were served in this tavern, which operated from 1785 to 1808.

SEE IT HERE!

MOUNT VERNON HOME AND GARDENS

George Washington and his wife, Martha, lived at Mount Vernon both before and after his presidency. Today, their magnificent home is the most frequently visited historic house in the nation. It has been fully restored and contains many pieces of Washington's original furniture. Washington suffered from poor teeth most of his life, and a set of his dentures is on display.

Visitors at Mount Vernon

Manassas

★ **Manassas National Battlefield:** Two Civil War battles—the First and Second Battles of Bull Run—were fought on this site. Plaques and maps explain the battles as you walk through the park.

Fredericksburg

★ **Mary Ball Washington House:** George Washington bought this small frame house for his mother, Mary Ball Washington, in 1772. On display are many original objects and pieces of furniture, including what Mary Washington called her "best dress china."

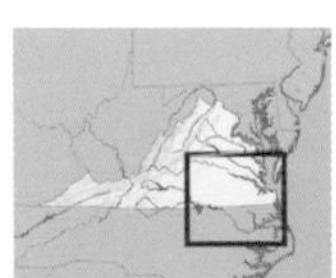

PIEDMONT

THINGS TO DO: See Thomas Jefferson's seven-day clock, taste Revolution-era food, and peer through the gunports at Fort Harrison.

Charlottesville

★ **Michie Tavern:** This 18th-century inn celebrates the music, dance, and food of that era. House rules such as "Boots not to be worn to bed" and "organ grinders [with monkeys] must sleep in the wash-house" are still posted on the walls.

Monticello

Orange

★ **Monticello:** Thomas Jefferson designed and lived in this hill-top house, which includes the first dome ever built on a North American house. Other unique features? A clock that shows the days of the week, and a pair of **dumbwaiters** that connect the wine cellar with the sitting room.

WORD TO KNOW

dumbwaiters *elevators for raising and lowering food and other items between floors*

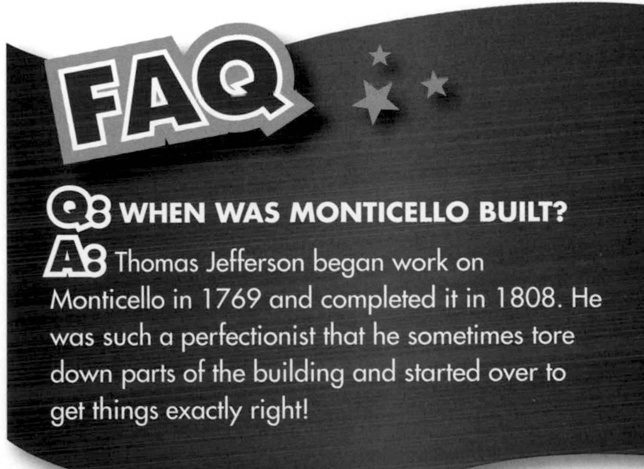

★ **Montpelier:** Montpelier was the home of James and Dolley Madison. The house has been restored to look as it did when the couple lived there.

Appomattox

★ **Appomattox Court House National Historical Park:** Here displays tell the story of the final day of the Civil War, when Confederate general Robert E. Lee surrendered to Union general Ulysses S. Grant.

Richmond

★ **Maymont Foundation:** Maymont is a 100-acre (40 ha) estate dating to the 19th century. On the grounds, you will find a nature center with wildlife exhibits, a farm with live animals, and a collection of carriages in a variety of styles.

★ **Chimborazo Medical Museum:** One of five military hospitals that operated in Virginia during the Civil War, Chimborazo is now a museum of early medicine. When you look at the drills, saws, and other equipment on display, it's hard to remember that all doctors swear an oath to "do no harm."

★ **Fort Harrison:** Early in the Civil War, Fort Harrison was a link in the chain of Confederate defenses. Union forces captured it in 1864.

★ **Museum and White House of the Confederacy:** This 1812 house was home to Confederate president Jefferson Davis and his family from 1861 to 1865. The house is furnished with many pieces that belonged to the Davises. Displays tell the story of the Civil War with pictures, documents, weapons, uniforms, and other memorabilia.

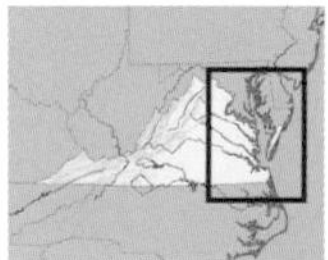

TIDEWATER

THINGS TO DO: Learn about Native American pottery, explore a battleship, and imagine what it was like at Jamestown.

King William County

★ **Pamunkey Indian Museum:** Through tools, pottery, clothing, and other artifacts, this museum traces the history of the region's Native people from the ice age to the present. Pamunkey women show visitors how their people have been making pottery for hundreds of years.

SEE IT HERE!

COLONIAL WILLIAMSBURG

Walk the streets of the town that served as Virginia's colonial capital from 1699 to 1780. Colonial Williamsburg is one of the nation's oldest living-history museums. Hundreds of buildings have been restored or reconstructed, including the Governor's Palace, the capitol, and the public hospital. You can visit shops where guides in period costumes demonstrate crafts such as barrel making, blacksmithing, and candle making.

A horse-drawn carriage in Colonial Williamsburg

Jamestown

★ **Jamestown Settlement:** Here you can walk through a re-created Powhatan village and watch costumed guides make arrows and tan hides. Nearby stands a replica of Jamestown's English fort. Women and men in period costumes show you how food was cooked and how the colonists defended themselves.

★ **Yorktown Victory Center:** Learn about the battle that decided the American Revolution at this museum, which depicts the lives of ordinary soldiers at a re-created army encampment.

Costumed interpreters at the Yorktown Victory Center

Norfolk

★ **Hampton Roads Naval Museum:** This museum traces the history of the U.S. Navy and features the restored World War II battleship *Wisconsin*.

EASTERN SHORE

THINGS TO DO: See wild ponies on Assateague Island, visit America's only oyster museum, and climb aboard an antique train.

Machipongo

★ **Barrier Islands Center:** This museum preserves the history of the now mostly deserted shore and islands.

Chincoteague Island

★ **Oyster and Maritime Museum:** The history of the men and women who harvested oysters on the Eastern Shore comes to life at this museum through words, pictures, and tools.

Parksley

★ **Eastern Shore Railway Museum:** With its town square, pillared porches, and old-time railway station, Parksley looks much as it did in 1885. The Railway Museum includes a luxury car from 1927, a 1949 caboose, and a 1950 sleeper car. All aboard!

Assateague Island

★ **Assateague Island National Seashore:** Wild ponies have roamed here since the 1700s. If you're lucky, you may see a stallion herding a band of mares and colts!

Ponies at Assateague Island National Seashore

SHENANDOAH VALLEY/BLUE RIDGE REGION

THINGS TO DO: Devour delicious food, check out George Washington's hair, and explore life on a plantation.

Ferrum

★ **Blue Ridge Institute and Farm Museum:** Here you can experience life on a German-American farm in 1800. You can sample sausage, stews, and pastries; see German folk dances; and try carding wool and dipping candles.

Winchester

★ **George Washington's Office Museum:** This reconstructed cabin marks the site of the office Washington used in 1756 when he worked as a surveyor. On display are surveying tools and early maps of the area, as well as a sample of Washington's hair.

★ **Museum of the Shenandoah Valley:** This restored pre–Civil War mansion is packed with paintings and Early American furniture. A highlight is a series of miniature rooms equipped with doll-size furnishings.

Steeles Tavern

★ **McCormick Farm and Workshop:** At this farm, Cyrus McCormick invented his mechanical reaper in 1831. On display are models of McCormick's machines and other examples of early farm equipment.

Lexington

★ **Natural Bridge:** Thomas Jefferson once owned this spectacular natural limestone bridge that spans a creek and links two mountains.

★ **Stonewall Jackson House:** This 1801 house has been restored to look much as it did when Jackson lived there before the Civil War.

Hardy

★ **Booker T. Washington National Monument:** Booker T. Washington spent his childhood as a slave on a small tobacco plantation at this site. The buildings of the Burroughs Plantation have been reconstructed, and costumed actors show how the enslaved people lived and worked.

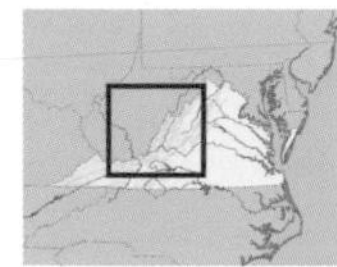

APPALACHIAN PLATEAU

THINGS TO DO: Hear great music, see a play, and learn about quilts, carving, and coal mining at the Appalachia Cultural Arts Center.

Hiltons

★ **Carter Family Fold:** A. P. Carter's general store is now a museum about the Carter Family and the history of country music. Weekly concerts are held nearby at a 1,000-seat music shed.

Appalachia

★ **Appalachia Cultural Arts Center:** Here you can see locally made arts and crafts, including quilts, ceramics, and wood carvings. Exhibits trace the history of coal mining in the region.

Abingdon

★ **Barter Theatre:** This theater opened during the Great Depression, when few people had cash to buy tickets. The theater let the people trade eggs, chickens, and other farm goods for entrance into the show.

A cabin at the Booker T. Washington National Monument

WRITING PROJECTS

Check out these ideas for creating a campaign brochure and writing you-are-there narratives. Or research the migration paths of settlers and explorers.

118

ART PROJECTS

You can illustrate the state song, create a dazzling PowerPoint presentation, or learn about the state quarter and design your own.

119

TIMELINE

What happened when? This timeline highlights important events in the state's history—and shows what was happening throughout the United States at the same time.

122

GLOSSARY

Remember the Words to Know from the chapters in this book? They're all collected here.

125

FAST FACTS

Use this section to find fascinating facts about state symbols, land area and population statistics, weather, sports teams, and much more.

126

WRITING PROJECTS

★ ★ ★

Write a Memoir, Journal, or Editorial for Your School Newspaper!

Picture Yourself . . .

★ Living in Jamestown in the 1600s. Imagine you are writing a letter to your friends back home in England. Describe what the village looks like. Who lives in Jamestown and how do they spend their days? What food do you grow and what kind of home do you have?

SEE: Chapter Three, pages 34–38.

GO TO: Sites such as www.nps.gov/jame/historyculture/jamestown-fact-sheets.htm and www.apva.org/history/index.html

★ As an abolitionist in the 1800s. What would you say to the plantation owners who wanted to keep enslaved people working in the fields? Would you help people held in slavery escape to the North? Or if you were enslaved, would you try to escape? What would you have to do to escape?

SEE: Chapter Four, pages 53–56.

GO TO: www.nps.gov/nr/travel/underground/

Brick maker in Jamestown

Create an interview script with a famous person from Virginia!

Research various famous Virginians, such as Ella Fitzgerald, Thomas Jefferson, Dolley Madison, Katherine Paterson, or Booker T. Washington.

Based on your research, pick one person you would most like to talk with.

Write a script of the interview. What questions would you ask? How would this person answer? Create a question-and-answer format. You may want to supplement this writing project with a voice-recording dramatization of the interview.

SEE: Chapters Six and Seven, pages 83–97, and the Biographical Dictionary, pages 133–136.

GO TO: www.virginia.org/site/features.asp?featureID=93

Compare and Contrast—When, Why, and How Did They Come?

Compare the migrations and explorations of Virginia's Native people and its first Europeans. Tell about:

★ When their migrations began
★ How they traveled
★ Why they migrated
★ Where their journeys began and ended
★ What they found when they arrived

SEE: Chapters Two and Three, pages 20–38.

ART PROJECTS

★ ★ ★

Create a PowerPoint Presentation or Visitors' Guide

Welcome to Virginia!

Virginia is a great place to visit and to live! From its natural beauty to its bustling cities and historical sites, there's plenty to see and do. In your PowerPoint presentation or brochure, highlight 10 to 15 of Virginia's amazing landmarks. Be sure to include:

★ a map of the state showing where these sites are located

★ photos, illustrations, Web links, natural history facts, geographic stats, climate and weather, plants and wildlife, and recent discoveries

SEE: Chapter One, pages 8–19, and Chapter Nine, pages 109–115.

GO TO: The Virginia travel site at www.virginia.org. Download and print maps, photos, national landmark images, and vacation ideas for tourists.

Create an Election Brochure or Web Site!

Run for office!

Throughout this book, you've read about some of the issues that concern Virginia today. As a candidate for governor of Virginia, create a campaign brochure or Web site. Explain how you meet the qualifications to be governor of Virginia. Talk about the three or four major issues you'll focus on if you're elected. Remember, you'll be responsible for Virginia's budget. How would you spend the taxpayers' money?

SEE: Chapter Seven, pages 90–97.

GO TO: Virginia's Government Web site at www.virginia.gov. You may also want to read some local newspapers. Try these:

Washington Post at www.washingtonpost.com

Virginian-Pilot at www.hamptonroads.com/pilotonline/

Richmond Times-Dispatch at www.timesdispatch.com/cva/ric/times_dispatch.html

Daily Progress (Charlottesville) www.dailyprogress.com/

Research Virginia's State Quarter

From 1999 to 2008, the U.S. Mint introduced new quarters commemorating each of the 50 states in the order that they were admitted to the Union. Each state's quarter features a unique design on its back, or reverse.

GO TO: www.usmint.gov/kids and find out what's featured on the back of the Virginia quarter.

★ Research the significance of the image.

★ What images would you choose for the reverse?

★ Make a poster showing the Virginia quarter and label each image.

SCIENCE, TECHNOLOGY, & MATH PROJECTS

Graph Population Statistics!

- ★ Compare population statistics (such as ethnic background, birth, death, and literacy rates) in Virginia counties or major cities.
- ★ In your graph or chart, look at population density and write sentences describing what the population statistics show; graph one set of population statistics and write a paragraph explaining what the graphs reveal.

SEE: Chapter Six, pages 77–79.

GO TO: The official Web site for the U.S. Census Bureau at www.census.gov and at http://quickfacts.census.gov/qfd/states/51000.html, to find out more about population statistics, how they work, and what the statistics are for Virginia.

Create a Weather Map of Virginia!

Use your knowledge of Virginia's geography to research and identify conditions that result in specific weather events. What is it about the geography of Virginia that makes it vulnerable to certain types of weather? Create a weather map or poster that shows the weather patterns over the state. Include a caption explaining the technology used to measure weather phenomena, and provide data.

SEE: Chapter One, pages 14–15.

GO TO: The National Oceanic and Atmospheric Administration's National Weather Service Web site at www.weather.gov for weather maps and forecasts for Virginia.

Delmarva Peninsula fox squirrel

Track Endangered Species

Using your knowledge of Virginia's wildlife, research what animals and plants are endangered or threatened.

- ★ Find out what the state is doing to protect these species.
- ★ Chart known populations of the animals and plants, and report on changes in certain geographic areas.

SEE: Chapter One, page 17.

GO TO: Web sites such as www.virginiaplaces.org/natural/especies.html

PRIMARY VS. SECONDARY SOURCES

★ ★ ★

What's the Diff?

Your teacher may require at least one or two primary sources and one or two secondary sources for your assignment. So, what's the difference between the two?

★ **Primary sources are original.** You are reading the actual words of someone's diary, journal, letter, autobiography, or interview. Primary sources can also be photographs, maps, prints, cartoons, news/film footage, posters, first-person newspaper articles, drawings, musical scores, and recordings. By the way, when you conduct a survey, interview someone, shoot a video, or take photographs to include in a project, you are creating primary sources!

★ **Secondary sources are what you find in encyclopedias, textbooks, articles, biographies, and almanacs.** These are written by a person or group of people who tell about something that happened to someone else. Secondary sources also recount what another person said or did. This book is an example of a secondary source.

Now that you know what primary sources are—where can you find them?

★ **Your school or local library:** Check the library catalog for collections of original writings, government documents, musical scores, and so on. Some of this material may be stored on microfilm. The Library of Congress Web site (www.loc.gov) is an excellent online resource for primary source materials.

★ **Historical societies:** These organizations keep historical documents, photographs, and other materials. Staff members can help you find what you are looking for. History museums are also great places to see primary sources firsthand.

★ **The Internet:** There are lots of sites that have primary sources you can download and use in a project or assignment.

TIMELINE

★ ★ ★

U.S. Events

BCE

Virginia Events

c. 15,000 BCE
The first people enter Virginia.

c. 12,000 BCE
The Archaic culture develops.

c. 1200 BCE
People begin settling in villages.

1400

1492
Christopher Columbus and his crew sight land in the Caribbean Sea.

1500

1584
Queen Elizabeth I of England asks Sir Walter Raleigh to start colonies in North America.

1600

c. 1600
Wahunsunacock unites 32 Powhatan groups.

The landing at Jamestown

1607
The first permanent English colony in North America is founded at Jamestown.

1619
The first Africans are brought to Virginia.

1620
Pilgrims found Plymouth Colony, the second permanent English settlement.

1682
René-Robert Cavelier, Sieur de La Salle, claims more than 1 million square miles (2.6 million sq km) of territory in the Mississippi River basin for France, naming it Louisiana.

1698
Virginia's capital moves from Jamestown to Middle Plantation, later renamed Williamsburg.

U.S. Events | 1700 | Virginia Events

1776 (U.S.)
Thirteen American colonies declare their independence from Great Britain.

1776 (Virginia)
Virginian Thomas Jefferson serves as the lead writer of the Declaration of Independence.

The surrender at Yorktown

1781 (Virginia)
The American Revolution ends at the Battle of Yorktown.

1787 (U.S.)
The U.S. Constitution is written.

1787 (Virginia)
Virginian James Madison serves as the lead author of the U.S. Constitution.

1788 (Virginia)
Virginia becomes the 10th state.

1800

1800 (Virginia)
Gabriel Prosser's plans for a slave revolt are discovered.

1803 (U.S.)
The Louisiana Purchase almost doubles the size of the United States.

1812–15 (U.S.)
The United States and Great Britain fight the War of 1812.

1831 (Virginia)
Nat Turner leads a slave uprising.

1846–48 (U.S.)
The United States fights a war with Mexico over western territories in the Mexican War.

1859 (Virginia)
Abolitionist John Brown leads a rebellion at Harpers Ferry.

John Brown

1861–65 (U.S.)
The American Civil War is fought between the Northern Union and the Southern Confederacy; it ends with the surrender of the Confederate army, led by General Robert E. Lee.

1861 (Virginia)
Virginia secedes from the Union; Richmond becomes the capital of the Confederate States of America; the Confederacy wins the First Battle of Manassas, the first major battle of the Civil War.

1862 (Virginia)
The first battle between ironclad ships is fought at Hampton Roads harbor.

U.S. Events

1863
President Abraham Lincoln frees all slaves in the Southern Confederacy with the Emancipation Proclamation.

1866
The U.S. Congress approves the Fourteenth Amendment to the U.S. Constitution, granting citizenship to African Americans.

1900

1917–18
The United States engages in World War I.

1929
The stock market crashes, plunging the United States more deeply into the Great Depression.

1941–45
The United States engages in World War II.

1951–53
The United States engages in the Korean War.

1964–73
The United States engages in the Vietnam War.

1991
The United States and other nations engage in the brief Persian Gulf War against Iraq.

2000

2001
Terrorists hijack four U.S. aircraft and crash them into the World Trade Center in New York City, the Pentagon in Arlington, Virginia, and a Pennsylvania field, killing thousands.

2003
The United States and coalition forces invade Iraq.

Virginia Events

1865
Confederate general Robert E. Lee surrenders at Appomattox Court House; Virginian John Wilkes Booth kills President Abraham Lincoln.

1870
Virginia is readmitted to the United States.

1917
Virginia shipyards produce ships for use in World War I.

1942
Virginia shipyards help rebuild the U.S. fleet after the Pearl Harbor attack.

1946
The U.S. Supreme Court rules that segregation on interstate buses is illegal, based on the case of Virginian Irene Morgan.

1958–64
Prince Edward County closes its public schools to avoid integrating them.

1990
L. Douglas Wilder is elected governor of Virginia, becoming the first African American governor in the United States.

L. Douglas Wilder

2001
Terrorists crash a plane into the Pentagon, killing 125 people.

2007
Virginia celebrates the 400th anniversary of the founding of Jamestown.

GLOSSARY

abolitionists people who were opposed to slavery and worked to end it

archaeologists people who study the remains of past human societies

breechcloth a garment worn by a man over his lower body

civil rights basic rights that are guaranteed to all people under the U.S. Constitution

commonwealth a government that works for the common good, or the common consent, of the people

constitution a written document that contains all the governing principles of a state or country

democracy government in which people choose their leaders

dulcimers musical instruments with three or four strings, traditionally played in the Appalachian region of the United States

dumbwaiters elevators for raising and lowering food and other items between floors

endangered in danger of becoming extinct

gross state product the total value of all the goods and services produced in a state

immunity natural protection against disease

indentured servants people who work for others under contract

integrate to bring together all members of society as equals

intelligence information gathering, spying

Parliament a governing body in certain countries (such as Great Britain), similar to the U.S. Congress

pesticides any chemicals or biological agents used to kill plant or animal pests

poll tax a fee that people must pay before they can vote

segregation separation from others, according to race, class, ethnic group, religion, or other factors

sharecroppers farmers who give a portion of their crops as rent for the land

stockade a fort built with walls of poles driven into the ground

synthetic related to something that doesn't occur in nature

threatened likely to become endangered in the foreseeable future

FAST FACTS

State Symbols

State seal

Statehood date June 25, 1788, the 10th state
Origin of state name Sir Walter Raleigh named the area Virginia in honor of Queen Elizabeth, the "Virgin Queen" of England
State capital Richmond
State nickname Old Dominion
State motto *Sic semper tyrannis* ("Thus Always to Tyrants")
State beverage Milk
State bird Cardinal
State floral emblem Dogwood
State dog Foxhound
State fish Brook trout
State folk dance Square dancing
State insect Tiger swallowtail butterfly
State song No official state song
State tree Dogwood
State fair Late September–early October at Richmond

Geography

Total area; rank 42,774 square miles (110,784 sq km); 35th
Land; rank 39,594 square miles (102,548 sq km); 37th
Water; rank 3,180 square miles (8,236 sq km); 15th
Inland water; rank 1,006 square miles (2,606 sq km); 22nd
Coastal water; rank 1,728 square miles (4,475 sq km); 5th
Territorial water; rank 446 square miles (1,155 sq km); 16th
Geographic center 5 miles (8 km) southwest of Buckingham
Longitude 75° 13′ W to 83° 37′ W
Latitude 36° 31′ N to 39° 37′ N
Highest point Mount Rogers, at 5,722 feet (1,744 m)
Lowest point Sea level along the Atlantic Ocean
Largest city Virginia Beach
Number of counties 95
Longest river James River, 340 miles (547 km)

Population

Population; rank (2006 estimate)	7,642,884; 12th
Density (2006 estimate)	193 persons per square mile (75 per sq km)
Population distribution (2000 census)	73% urban, 27% rural
Ethnic distribution (2005 estimate)	White persons: 73.6%*
	Black persons: 19.9%*
	Asian persons: 4.6%*
	American Indian and Alaska Native persons: 0.3%*
	Native Hawaiian and Other Pacific Islander: 0.3%*
	Persons reporting two or more races: 1.6%
	Persons of Hispanic or Latino origin: 6.0%†
	White persons not Hispanic: 68.2%

** Includes persons reporting only one race.*

† Hispanics may be of any race, so they are also included in applicable race categories.

Weather

Record high temperature	110°F (43°C) at Columbia on July 5, 1900, and Balcony Falls on July 15, 1954
Record low temperature	–30°F (–34°C) at Monterey on February 10, 1899, and Mountain Lake Biological Station on January 22, 1985
Average July temperature	78°F (26°C)
Average January temperature	36°F (2°C)
Average yearly precipitation	43 inches (109 cm)

State flag

STATE SONG

At present, Virginia has no official state song. "Oh Shenandoah," a popular folk song from the 19th century, refers to the Shenandoah Valley of western Virginia. Some Virginia legislators have suggested making it the state song.

Oh Shenandoah

Oh, Shenandoah, I long to hear you,
Away, you rolling river
Oh, Shenandoah, I long to hear you
Away, I'm bound away, cross the wide Missouri.

Oh, Shenandoah, I love your daughter,
Away, you rolling river
Oh, Shenandoah, I love your daughter
Away, I'm bound away, cross the wide Missouri.

Oh, Shenandoah, I'm bound to leave you,
Away, you rolling river
Oh, Shenandoah, I'm bound to leave you
Away, I'm bound away, cross the wide Missouri.

Oh, Shenandoah, I long to see you,
Away, you rolling river
Oh, Shenandoah, I long to see you
Away, I'm bound away, cross the wide Missouri.

NATURAL AREAS AND HISTORIC SITES

National Parks

Virginia boasts five national parks, including *Shenandoah National Park* in the Blue Ridge Mountains; *Great Falls National Park; Prince William Forest National Park*, the biggest protected forest and natural region in the Washington, D.C., area; *Theodore Roosevelt Island National Park*; and *Wolf Trap National Park for the Performing Arts.*

National Scenic Trails and National Historic Trails

Two national scenic trails pass through Virginia: the *Appalachian National Scenic Trail*, a trail through the Appalachian Mountains; and the *Potomac Heritage National Scenic Trail.* The state features two national historic trails, including the *Overmountain Victory National Historic Trail* and the *Captain John Smith Chesapeake National Historic Trail*, the country's first national water trail.

National Battlefield Parks and National Military Park

Virginia's four national battlefield parks include *Manassas National Battlefield Park, Petersburg National Battlefield, Richmond National Battlefield Park*, and *Yorktown Battlefield. Fredericksburg and Spotsylvania National Military Park* is the largest military park in the world.

National Historic Sites and National Historical Parks

The state features two national historic sites, including *Jamestown National Historic Site* and *Maggie L. Walker National Historic Site*, which honors the first woman to start a bank and serve as a bank president in the United States. Virginia has three national historical parks, including *Appomattox Court House National Historical Park* and *Cedar Creek & Belle Grove National Historical Park.*

National Memorial and National Monuments

Virginia is home to the *Robert E. Lee Memorial*, or *Arlington House*, and two national monuments, the *Booker T. Washington National Monument* and the *George Washington Birthplace National Monument.*

National Seashore

Assateague Island National Seashore covers 18,000 acres (7,200 ha) in Virginia and Maryland.

National Forests

The *George Washington National Forest* and the *Jefferson National Forest* cover thousands of acres along the state's western and northwestern borders.

State Parks

Virginia's state park system includes 34 beautiful state parks and recreation areas, including *False Cape State Park, Grayson Highlands State Park*, and *Douthat State Park.*

SPORTS TEAMS

NCAA Teams (Division I)

College of William and Mary *Tribe*
George Mason University *Patriots*
Hampton University *Pirates*
James Madison University *Dukes*
Liberty University *Flames*
Longwood University *Lancers*
Norfolk State University *Spartans*
Old Dominion University *Monarchs*
Radford University *Highlanders*
University of Richmond *Spiders*
University of Virginia *Cavaliers*
Virginia Commonwealth University *Rams*
Virginia Military Institute *Keydets*
Virginia Polytechnic Institute & State University *Gobblers/Hokies*

Virginia Tech Hokies

CULTURAL INSTITUTIONS

Libraries

Jefferson-Madison Regional Library (main branch in Charlottesville) provides service to the city of Charlottesville, Thomas Jefferson's home county of Albemarle, and three more counties. This public library dates back to the private libraries of Jefferson, James Monroe, and other Virginians.

The *Library of Virginia* (Richmond) was built in 1823 and has a vast collection of materials on Virginia's history. The library also sponsors many events and exhibitions relating to Virginia.

Museums

The *Black History Museum and Cultural Center* (Richmond) holds works by renowned artists such as Sam Gilliam, John Biggers, and P. H. Polk. In addition, the museum has an extensive collection of African artifacts and textiles from various ethnic groups throughout Africa.

The *Chrysler Museum of Art* (Norfolk) is home to 30,000 objects spanning nearly 5,000 years of history. Highlights include European and American painting and sculpture, a world-renowned glass collection, a rich photography program, and Art Nouveau furniture, as well as African, Asian, Egyptian, Pre-Columbian, and Islamic art.

The *Poe Museum* (Richmond) provides a retreat into early 19th-century Richmond where Edgar Allan Poe lived and worked. The museum documents his accomplishments with pictures, relics, and verse, focusing on his many years in the city.

The *Virginia Air & Space Center* (Hampton) features dozens of hands-on air and space exhibits, a premiere interactive gallery that spans 100 years of flight, more than 30 historic aircraft, and unique spaceflight artifacts.

The *Virginia Historical Society* (Richmond) has been open for 175 years and has thousands of pieces in its exhibits.

The *Virginia Museum of Natural History* (Martinsville) has many collections dating from Virginia's prehistoric years to the present day. It also has a new collection of 11 million insects from Virginia, which the Smithsonian Institution donated.

Performing Arts

Virginia has two opera companies, two symphony orchestras, and one dance company.

Universities and Colleges

In 2006, there were 39 public and 71 private institutions of higher learning.

ANNUAL EVENTS

January–March

Highland County Maple Sugar Festival in Monterey (March)

Garden Symposium in Williamsburg (late March or early April)

April–June

Dogwood Festival in Charlottesville (late April)

International Azalea Festival in Norfolk (late April)

Virginia Gold Cup in The Plains (early May)

Shenandoah Apple Blossom Festival in Winchester (early May)

Jamestown Landing Day in Williamsburg (May)

Harborfest in Norfolk (early June)

Boardwalk Art Show in Virginia Beach (late June)

Hampton Jazz Festival (late June)

July–September

Annual Statler Brothers Independence Day Celebration in Staunton (July)

The Big Gig in Richmond (July)

Scottish Games and Gathering of the Clans in Alexandria (July)

Highlands Arts and Crafts Festival in Abingdon (first two weeks in August)

Old Fiddler's Convention in Galax (August)

Neptune Festival in Virginia Beach (late September)

October–December

Danville Harvest Jubilee (October)

Oyster Festival on Chincoteague Island (October)

Olde Towne Ghostwalk in Portsmouth (late October)

Blue Ridge Folklife Festival in Ferrum (fourth Saturday in October)

The Grand Illumination in Colonial Williamsburg (early December)

BIOGRAPHICAL DICTIONARY

Arthur Ashe See page 89.

Pearl Bailey (1918–1990), born in Newport News, was a singer, Broadway actor, and author.

Ronde and **Tiki Barber (1975–)** are twin brothers who were born in Roanoke. Both went on to play football in the NFL, and they have written children's books together.

George Caleb Bingham (1811–1879) was an artist born in Augusta County. He often depicted frontier life on the Missouri River.

John Wilkes Booth (1838–1865) was a popular actor who settled in Virginia in 1858. In 1865, he shot and killed President Abraham Lincoln.

Carter Braxton (1736–1797), born in Newington, was a delegate to the Continental Congress and a signer of the Declaration of Independence.

Tiki (left) and Ronde Barber

Katie Couric

Harry F. Byrd See page 67.

Richard Evelyn Byrd (1888–1957), born in Winchester, was an Arctic and Antarctic explorer.

William Byrd II (1674–1744) was born on a James River plantation and founded the city of Richmond.

Alvin Pleasant (A. P.) Carter (1891–1960) of Maces Springs formed the Carter Family singers. The Carters awakened national interest in country music.

William Clark (1770–1838), born in Caroline County, explored territory acquired through the Louisiana Purchase from 1803 to 1806.

Katie Couric (1957–) is a broadcast journalist who has cohosted the *Today* show and anchors the *CBS Evening News*. She was born in Arlington.

Rita Dove (1952–) is a poet who teaches at the University of Virginia. From 1993 to 1995, she was poet laureate of the United States.

Charles Richard Drew (1904–1950) was a medical researcher who found a way to store plasma, the life-giving substance in blood. A native of Arlington, he helped establish the Red Cross Blood Bank.

Missy Elliott (1971–) is a singer who was born and raised in Portsmouth. She is known for the feisty spirit on albums such as *Da Real World*.

Moses Jacob Ezekiel (1844–1917) was a sculptor born in Richmond. He created the monument to the Confederate dead in Arlington National Cemetery.

Ella Fitzgerald See page 87.

Nikki Giovanni (1943–) teaches at Virginia Tech in Blacksburg and writes poetry and picture books for children, as well as works for adult readers.

Nikki Giovanni

Missy Elliott

Ellen Glasgow (1874–1945) was a novelist who wrote about Virginia history and society. She was born in Richmond.

William Henry Harrison See page 97.

Patrick Henry (1736–1799), born in Hanover County, was a member of the Virginia House of Burgesses and a delegate to the First and Second Continental Congresses. He rallied people to the Revolution with the words, "Give me liberty or give me death!"

Oliver W. Hill See page 70.

Thomas "Stonewall" Jackson See page 59.

Thomas Jefferson See pages 45 and 97.

John Paul Jones (1747–1792), who settled in Fredericksburg in 1773, commanded the ship *Bonhomme Richard* during a battle with the British in the American Revolution. When ordered to surrender, he replied, "I have not yet begun to fight."

John Mercer Langston See page 65.

Francis Lightfoot Lee (1734–1797) of Westmoreland County was a signer of the Declaration of Independence and a delegate to the First Continental Congress.

Richard Henry Lee (1732–1794), born in Westmoreland County, was a delegate to the Continental Congress and a signer of the Declaration of Independence.

Robert E. Lee See page 56.

Meriwether Lewis (1774–1809) of Albemarle County explored territory acquired through the Louisiana Purchase from 1803 to 1806.

Dolley Madison See page 51.

James Madison See page 97.

John Marshall See page 94.

Dave Matthews (1967–) is a musician who was born in South Africa. He eventually moved to Charlottlesville, where his band originated, and he owns farmland in Scottsville.

Cyrus Hall McCormick See page 107.

Dave Matthews

Alonzo Mourning

Robert Mills See page 83.

James Monroe See page 97.

Alonzo Mourning (1970–) is a professional basketball player for the Miami Heat. He was born in Chesapeake.

Jerome Myers (1867–1940) was a painter and draftsman from Petersburg. He often made paintings and drawings of immigrant life in New York City.

Katherine Paterson See page 85.

Mary Peake See page 55.

Pocahontas (1595?–1618) was the daughter of a Powhatan chief. She helped bring about peace between the American Indians and colonists when she married John Rolfe in 1614.

Edgar Allan Poe (1809–1849) was a poet and short-story writer, now considered the founder of the modern detective story. He was raised in Richmond.

Walter Reed (1851–1902) was a U.S. Army medical officer born in Belroi. He made major discoveries about how typhoid and yellow fever are spread.

John Rolfe (1585?–1622) was one of the early Jamestown colonists. He introduced tobacco to Virginia as a cash crop.

Winfield Scott (1786–1866), born near Petersburg, was a hero of the War of 1812 and served as general in chief of the U.S. Army from 1841 to 1861.

John Smith See page 36.

Zachary Taylor See page 97.

John Tyler See page 97.

Edward Virginius Valentine (1838–1930) was a sculptor from Richmond who made statues of Thomas Jefferson and Stonewall Jackson, among many others.

Wahunsunacock See page 28.

Tom Wolfe

Booker T. Washington

Maggie Lena Walker See page 103.

Booker T. Washington (1856–1915) was born into slavery in Franklin County. He became a writer, speaker, and educator who helped to found the Tuskegee Institute in Alabama for the education of African American students.

George Washington See pages 44 and 97.

L. Douglas Wilder See page 97.

Woodrow Wilson See page 97.

Tom Wolfe (1931–) is a journalist and novelist born in Richmond. His books include *The Right Stuff* and *The Bonfire of the Vanities*.

Elliott Yamin (1978–) is a singer who gained fame during the *American Idol* competition, coming in third in 2006. Born in Los Angeles, he spent most of his youth in Richmond.

RESOURCES

BOOKS

Nonfiction

Aronson, Marc. *Sir Walter Ralegh and the Quest for El Dorado*. New York: Clarion Books, 2000.

Bernstein, Richard B. *Thomas Jefferson: The Revolution of Ideas*. New York: Oxford University Press, 2004.

Cressey, Pamela J., and Margaret J. Anderson. *Alexandria, Virginia*. New York: Oxford University Press, 2006.

Edwards, Judith. *Nat Turner's Slave Rebellion in American History*. Berkeley Heights, N.J.: Enslow, 2000.

Fradin, Dennis. *Jamestown, Virginia*. New York: Benchmark, 2007.

Fritz, Jean. *The Double Life of Pocahontas*. New York: Putnam, 1983.

Fritz, Jean. *The Great Little Madison*. New York: Putnam, 1998.

Fritz, Jean. *The Lost Colony of Roanoke*. New York: Putnam, 2004.

Harkins, Susan Sales, and William H. Harkins. *Colonial Virginia*. Hockessin, Del.: Mitchell Lane, 2007.

O'Brien, Patrick. *Duel of the Ironclads: The Monitor vs. the Virginia*. New York: Walker, 2007.

Pobst, Sandy. *Voices from Colonial America: Virginia, 1607–1776*. Washington, D.C.: National Geographic, 2005.

Fiction

Denenberg, Barry. *When Will This Cruel War Be Over?: The Civil War Diary of Emma Simpson, Gordonsville, Virginia, 1864*. New York: Scholastic Inc., 1996.

Elliott, Laura. *Give Me Liberty*. New York: Katherine Tegen Books, 2006.

Kudlinski, Kathleen. *My Lady, Pocahontas*. Tarrytown, N.Y.: Marshall Cavendish, 2006.

McKissack, Patricia C. *A Picture of Freedom: The Diary of Clotee, a Slave Girl, Belmont Plantation, Virginia 1859*. New York: Scholastic Inc., 2003.

DVDs

Discoveries—America: Virginia. Bennett Watt Media, 2004.
The New World: Nightmare in Jamestown. National Geographic Video, 2005.
Pocahontas: Ambassador of the New World. A&E Home Video, 2005.
Thomas Jefferson: Philosopher of Freedom. A&E Home Video, 2004.

WEB SITES AND ORGANIZATIONS

Commonwealth of Virginia
www.virginia.org
Virginia's official Web site offers tons of information about government, travel, and history. Don't forget to visit the kids' page.

The Library of Virginia
www.lva.lib.va.us/whatwedo/k12/vhr/index.htm
A great resource for teachers and students, the library provides an array of links about all periods of Virginia history.

Virginia Black History Archives
www.library.vcu.edu/jbc/speccoll/vbha/vbhalink.html
This site provides many links to Internet resources on African American history and culture.

Virginia Historical Society
www.vahistorical.org
To find in-depth information about Virginia's history.

Virginia's Indians, Past & Present
falcon.jmu.edu/~ramseyil/vaindians.htm
To find detailed information about Virginia's Native American nations.

INDEX

★ ★ ★

AUTHOR'S TIPS AND SOURCE NOTES

★ ★ ★

When researching a topic, I find it is most useful to begin by reading full-length histories and taking extensive notes. Then I begin exploring Web sites to gather current information. Several books on Virginia proved particularly valuable in my research for this book. Among them are *Virginia Reconsidered: New Histories of the Old Dominion*, edited by Kevin R. Hardwick and Warren R. Hofstra; *Virginia: A Commonwealth Comes of Age*, by Lisa Antonelli; *Forced Founders: Indians, Debtors, Slaves, and the Making of the American Revolution in Virginia*, by Woody Holton; *Virginia: The Old Dominion*, by Matthew Andrews; and *Civil War Virginia: Battlefield for a Nation*, by James I. Robinson. A useful Web site was marg.mhost.com/vahistory.html, which has links to an enormous variety of sites related to the state.

Photographs © 2009: Alamy Images: 90, 91 left (Rob Crandall/SCPhotos), 110 right (David R. Frazier Photolibrary, Inc.), 111 (Oliver Gerhard/imagebroker), 75 right, 80 bottom, 82, 115 (Jeff Greenberg); Animals Animals/Michael Gadomski: 12; AP Images: 85 (Kirkland), 5 top right, 63 bottom, 67, 68, 71; Architect of the Capitol, Washington, DC: 45 bottom, 123 top; Art Resource, NY: 49 bottom, 56 (Edward Caledon Bruce/National Portrait Gallery, Smithsonian Institution, Washington, DC), 25 (Werner Forman), 29 (Giraudon), 26 (Mingei International Museum), 44 left (Charles Willson Peale/Yale University Art Gallery, New Haven, Connecticut), 62 bottom, 65 (Schomburg Center), 4 top right, 27, 41, 66 (The New York Public Library); Bridgeman Art Library International Ltd., London/New York: 51 (Aline Alaux/Collection of the New-York Historical Society), 21 bottom, 28 (Bibliotheque des Arts Decoratifs, Paris, France/Archives Charmet), 32 top, 33 top left, 36, 122 (Private Collection), 50 (Private Collection/Archives Charmet), 59 (Private Collection/Peter Newark Military Pictures); Buddy Mays/Travel Stock/Tom & Michelle Grimm: 5 bottom, 113 right; Corbis Images: 24, 32 bottom, 40, 45 top, 60, 63 top right, 64, 70, 87 top (Bettmann), 135 bottom (Laura Farr/zuma), 43 (Francis G. Mayer), 100, 101 left (Roger Ressmeyer), 17 top (Lynda Richardson), 47 (Junius Brutus Stearns/Bettmann), back cover (Gilbert Stuart/Christie's Images), 30 (The Mariners' Museum), 97, 124 (Tim Wright), 48 bottom, 54, 58, 123 bottom; Danita Delimont Stock Photography/Maresa Pryor: 8, 9 left; Digital Railroad/Ariel Skelley/Blend Images: 101 right, 103 bottom; Everett Collection, Inc.: 133 bottom (Andrew Eccles), 86, 136 top; Getty Images: 89 top (David Ashdown), 135 top (Victor Baldizon), 88, 130 center (Kevin C. Cox), 73 (Chris Jackson), 134 top (Peter Kramer), 76 (O. Louis Mazzatenta), 87 bottom, 136 bottom (Frank Micelotta), 35, 37, 118 (MPI), 44 right (Richard Nowitz), 134 bottom (Mike Simons), cover inset (Medford Taylor), 48 top, 49 top left (The Bridgeman Art Library); iStockphoto: 116 bottom, 130 bottom (Geoffrey Black), 91 right, 93 (DoxaDigitalImaging), 130 top (David Freund), 128 (Vladislav Lebedinski), 19 (Frank Leung), 33 bottom; JupiterImages: 84, 121; Landov, LLC/John Angelillo/UPI: 133 top; Library of Congress: 62 top, 63 top left (Joseph Becker), 61 (Frances Benjamin Johnston), 5 top left, 49 top right, 57 (Kurz & Allison); Masterfile/Garry Black: cover main; Courtesy of Michigan State University Library: 55; Minden Pictures/Tim Fitzharris: 114; National Geographic Image Collection: 21 top right, 22 top (Roy Andersen), 110 left (Annie Griffiths Belt), 13, 20 top, 21 top left (Kenneth Garrett); National Museum of the American Indian, Smithsonian Institution: 20 bottom, 22 bottom; Courtesy of National Park Service/Maggie L. Walker National Historic Site: 103 top; North Wind Picture Archives: 107; Photo Researchers, NY: 94 (Henry Inman), 4 top left, 17 bottom, 120 (Samuel R. Maglione); PhotoEdit/Jeff Greenberg: 78; Phototake/Kenneth J. Stein, Ph.D.: 9 right, 15; Photri Inc.: 74, 75 left (J. Greenberg), 89 bottom (R. Simpson); Robertstock.com: 113 left (K. Rice), 102 (Ariel Skelley); StockFood, Inc.: 81 bottom (Beatriz Da Costa), 4 bottom, 80 top (Studio Schmitz); The Granger Collection, New York: 33 top right, 38, 52, 83; The Image Works/Stan Walker/Syracuse Newspapers: 81 top; TIPS Images/Glowimages Inc.: 18; US Mint: 116 top, 119; Vector-Images.com: 98, 99, 126, 127.

Maps by Map Hero, Inc.